THE HOWARD STERN BOOK

THE HOWARD STERN BOOK

An **Un**authorized, **Un**abashed, **Un**censored Fan's Guide

by Jim Cegielski

A Citadel Press Book
Published by Carol Publishing Group

A Citadel Press Book
Published by Carol Publishing Group
Citadel Press is a registered trademark of Carol Communications, Inc.
Editorial Offices: 600 Madison Avenue, New York, N.Y. 10022
Sales and Distribution Offices: 120 Enterprise Avenue, Secaucus, N.J. 07094
In Canada: Canadian Manda Group, P.O. Box 920, Station U, Toronto,
Ontario M8Z 5P9

Queries regarding rights and permissions should be addressed to Carol
Publishing Group, 600 Madison Avenue, New York, N.Y. 10022
Carol Publishing Group books are available at special discounts for bulk pur-
chases, sales promotions, fund-raising, or educational purposes. Special editions
can be created to specifications. For details, contact Special Sales Department,
Carol Publishing Group, 120 Enterprise Avenue, Secaucus, N.J. 07094

Manufactured in the United States of America

10 9 8 7 6 5 4 3 2 1

Designed by Andrew B. Gardner

Library of Congress Cataloging-in-Publication Data

Cegielski, Jim, 1963-
    The Howard Stern book : an unauthorized, unabashed, uncensored fan's
guide / Jim Cegielski; introduction by "Grandpa" Al Lewis.
        p. cm.
    "A Citadel Press book."
    ISBN 0-8065-1505-8
    1. Stern, Howard, 1954-. 2. Radio broadcasters—United States—Biography.
I. Title.
PN1991.4.S82C45 1994
791.44'028'092—dc20
    [B]   93-43798
                                                                              CIP

Dedication

In loving memory of my father, who taught me that there isn't anything wrong with laughing at a Polish joke (as long as it's funny).

CONTENTS

CONTENTS

FOREWORD

n the year 2094, when
they open the time capsule, people will say "What is a Howard
Stern?" To make it easier for them to come up with an answer, I
will be their Rosetta stone. As the great Oscar Wilde said,
"Nothing succeeds like excess." Our dear Howard is just full of
excess, and a lot of other things—talent, chutzpah, gall, and the
tenacity of a Jewish locust. Howard is a poor man's tummeler, a
nudnick, and a shtupper (consult your O.E.D. for definitions of
the above). I, Al Lewis, have always enjoyed being a guest of
Howard's (on NBC and KCOC, his Saturday syndicated show,
his Nassau Coliseum live show, Channel 9 TV, and his
Channel 5 Fox TV show).

I am often asked, "What is Howard like?" He is a nice
Jewish boy gone astray, a terrible tennis player, a wonderful
family man and father. The smartest man in Howard's lineage
was his grandfather, who, knowing his family very well, would
greet them by saying, "Where is my money?" Howard, I love
you, but in those immortal words, *Where is my money?*

Al Lewis
September 1993

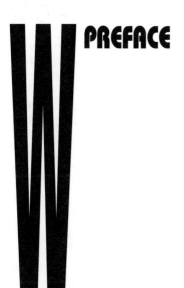

PREFACE

hy the hell did I write this book?

Two reasons, actually. The first is that I was sick and tired of reading and hearing only negative comments about Mr. Stern. Here is a guy who entertains millions of fans every day; he must be doing something right.

The second, and more important, reason is to defend Howard's right to speak his mind over the public airwaves, whether you agree with him or not. Unfortunately, there are a lot of people who want to take away his First Amendment right to do so. Frighteningly, some of these people are in positions of power.

And while I'm at it, I want to give Howard's fans, who range from business executives to janitors to Hollywood's elite, a definitive "guide" to Mr. Stern for their pleasure and amusement.

There are people who may consider themselves Howard Haters, but it's probably only because they tuned in to his show briefly, happened to hear him say something offensive, and turned the dial immediately. I was once part of this group. And I want to say to these people that you can still easily be converted, you too can become a Stern fan, or even fanatic. You just need to do the following:

1. Realize that Howard is a family man and not the second coming of Satan.

2. Turn your radio dial back to Howard's station and give him another chance. Howard offends everyone at some point; don't take it personally. If you listen without prejudice, you'll find out that he is one of the funniest, most thought-provoking, and most talented people in all of the entertainment industry.

3. Realize that when you listen to Howard Stern, you're supporting the First Amendment to our Constitution. There are a lot of people with little minds out there who believe you are not capable of deciding for yourself what you should or should not hear. They probably also feel you're incapable of raising your children in a responsible manner.

I have found that the longer you listen to Howard's morning show, the better it gets. Howard draws you into his life through the broadcast; you actually begin to care about the fact that Howard was unable to have sex with his wife last night or that Richard Simmons came over for dinner.

I remember the first time I heard Howard call his mother on the show. Howard was calling her to complain about the fact that she used to wash the stains out of his underwear in the bathroom sink and leave them there to soak so that everyone could see them. All of us have had embarrassing childhood experiences, especially when it comes to our parents. Most of us would never confront our parents about them, even in private; only Howard would do so in front of millions of people on the radio. Call me a voyeur, but I'm sure I am not alone when I tell you the interaction between Howard and his mother is some of the funniest and most interesting conversation ever broadcast on radio.

Howard's personal life is actually a part of the show. You meet his father (Howard will never let him forget that tape on which Ben Stern yelled at a seven-year-old Howard, "Shut up! Sit down!"), his sister, his wife and children, and even his old girlfriends. If you have ever had any type of personal relationship with Howard, you and your life are ripe for discussion on his show.

It's no different with Howard himself. He tells us everything—and I mean everything—about himself. If you listen regularly to Howard, then you know that he masturbates—often. A lot of you are probably now asking, "Why does he feel it necessary to tell us about this little matter?" (Pardon the pun—no reference to his underendowed anatomy intended.) I think it's because Howard likes to point out the hypocrisy that we are so used to in our daily lives. We all masturbate (at least those of us who are males do), but God forbid that anyone should actually *admit* to it. It's also funny knowing that there are Howard Haters listening to his show who will be offended by the fact that he admits to an act that every other red-blooded male over the age of twelve has performed at some time in his life. As a matter of fact, I'm sure some of the most offended and vocal Howard Haters call the station to complain about Howard's masturbation bit and then hang up the phone so they can whack off while looking at the latest issue of *Hustler*.

It is all a matter of being honest with oneself and of being able to laugh at oneself. Howard is just like the rest of us, whether you like it or not. I honestly believe that the biggest Howard Haters are those people who are afraid to admit to the very things Howard discusses so openly.

Let's face it: Howard is brutally honest about life. One of the biggest criticisms of Howard is his reliance on toilet humor. Well, I think it is sign of comedic genius that he can take a topic like the use of the toilet and make it funny. That brings me to the "Courtesy Flush." For those of you who insist that no one can take the act of going to the bathroom and make it funny, you never heard Howard preach the virtues of the "Courtesy Flush."

It is quite simple: When you're in a public rest room and

doing your duty, do not sit there and revel in the smell of your own excrement; the guy in the next stall may not be enjoying it quite as much as you. This is the time for a "Courtesy Flush," while you're finishing up what you need to do. Remember, it never hurts to flush twice. This is good common sense, courtesy of Howard Stern. It's just a bit funnier because Howard had to tell us this over nationally syndicated airwaves.

Okay, I'll admit that these are the kinds of bits that earned Howard the much-overused titles of "Radio Bad Boy" and "Shock Jock." But he has other talents. He is an incredible comedian and interviewer. He combines an extremely quick wit with the ability to push each of his guests to the limit. And most guests reveal some deep, dark secret to Howard before they ever realize they're also revealing it to millions of rabid listeners.

For years, the media has called this man a flash in the pan, a fad that will soon die, or a bad dream that will soon be over. They were writing this in papers back in the early 1980s. Howard's own book, *Private Parts*, changed all of that. When *Private Parts* shot up to number one on the *New York Times* and *Publishers Weekly* bestseller lists, it became clear that Howard's popularity is not waning, but is in fact, growing by leaps and bounds.

The reason the media had been so far off base about Howard is because they saw him as the "Shock Jock," and nothing else. If that were really what Howard was all about, he would have been a bad memory long ago. The only way Howard could have lasted this long, and become a huge success with such a loyal following, is that Mr. Howard Stern is a master of the talk radio format. Actually, a better description would be that he is like the Beatles of talk radio. He has changed the radio industry by creating an entirely new type of talk radio. He rarely plays music, unless it is a song parody or to satisfy a guest who's plugging a new album. (Even then, Howard chats through every snippet of song he plays.) He simply talks to us for four and a half to five hours each weekday morning, and we love him because he makes us laugh and keeps our attention during that hellish period in the morning known as "drivetime."

We shouldn't give him all the credit, however; Howard does have some help. Robin Quivers, Jackie Martling, Fred Norris, Gary Dell'Abate, and John Melendez are a very talented team to work with. But there is no question whose brains are behind the glorious radio show, the ground-breaking TV show, and the other special projects this group puts together. I hope that Howard and his crew enjoy this book as much as I know his fans will.

Howard's creativity and productivity are phenomenal. He has entertained us on the radio, on television, and in videos for over a decade. Many of those performances were hilarious. However, it has not been possible for me to include all, or even most, of them in this book. I have had to select my own personal favorites from the many Stern shows. I'm sure some of you will find that I should have selected other memorable moments. I only wish I had been able to incorporate every one of them.

ACKNOWLEDGMENTS

I am very grateful to many people for the successful completion of this book. First and foremost is Richard J. Pilch. I could never thank him enough for all of his help with the research, writing, and revisions in regards to this project. I especially want to thank him for his kind words about my writing and his unabashed and uncensored support of this work.

I'd also like to thank my editor, Eileen Schlesinger Cotton; my agent, Bert Holtje; and attorneys, Mel Wulf and Henry Kaufman. I would also like to thank Mike Lewis for all his insightful additions.

There are many others who helped and supported me in the arduous task that this book became. Many thanks to Kathy C. and Fran Pilch for being there when I needed them. My gratitude also goes out to fellow Stern followers John Cunningham, Scott Watrous, Tom Korman, and Charlie Young. More thanks to Tom Trulis, Matt Knoster, Marjorie Smith, Jon Anderson, Jay Hyde, Chuck Dresner, and Tom Cox. Thanks also to my brothers, Mike and Don, my sister, Tammy, and to Rich and Lance Pilch. A very special thank you to Gary Gentel, who was one of the few who actually encouraged me to write. Many, many thanks to "Grampa" Al Lewis for writing the foreword; the original Munsters is the only Munsters, as far as I'm concerned. Finally, thanks to my family, Carolyn, Emily, and Alison, for putting up with my nonstop Howard Stern listening, watching, talking, laughing, and typing over many a night and weekend. Oh, and thanks, Howard—you're the best!

HOWARD STERN, THE MAN, THE LEGEND

1 CHAPTER

FROM BABY TO BROADCASTER

played the "Shut up! Sit down!" tape on the air, Ben called in and told Howard, "I now know how Richard Nixon felt."

Over the years, Ben has made some radio appearances on Howard's show, and I'm happy to report that he seems to have mellowed with the years. (Perhaps it's the lack of sex that Howard reports his father suffers.) However, Ben still makes it pretty obvious to everyone who has heard him that Howard inherited his sense of humor from his mother, Ray Stern. Ray is a pleasure to listen to whenever she appears on the radio show. She has a warmth about her that carries over the airwaves no matter what topic she is discussing with her dear son Howard.

A couple of years back, Howard found out that his mother had been discussing the size of his penis with his sister, Ellen. Howard called up his mother to confront her, and the resulting conversation was a perfect demonstration of the humor Ray Stern passed along to her youngest offspring.

In response to Howard's questioning about why she had told Ellen that his "wiener" wasn't very big, Ray explained, "We were discussing your show and you're always alluding to it, and I said, 'You know, I think he's right.'" She didn't remember it being anything special, she said. Howard tried to discredit his mother's response by pointing out to her that she hadn't seen him naked since she'd stopped taking his temperature. When was that? "I think you must have been about twenty-five years old," Ray answered. Score one for Mom.

Howard, concerned that people would suspect that he hadn't been joking about the size of his genitals all these years, continued his interrogation. He wanted to know why his mother and sister discussed his penis, but not Ellen's husband's. "You're my baby boy . . . you're my little boy," replied Ray. "Your *very* little boy!" interjected Robin.

Sticking with his penis line of questioning, Howard wanted to know why his father's was so big. "Who said he was big? And compared to who?" Ray asked. "Compared to me," came Howard's reply. "Compared to you," Ray repeated, and broke up laughing. Score two for Mom. Now we know why Howard sometimes seems a bit insecure, and where he got that biting sense of humor.

No one can handle Howard like his mother can. She seems to be the only person who can battle Howard sentence for sentence, and even stand a chance of coming out even with him. This guy has made other radio personalities look like total wimps when it comes to verbal warfare, but Howard's mother always comes out sounding golden after doing battle with her former protégé. And no matter how steamed up their phone conversations get, Howard virtually always closes with, "I love you, Mommy."

Getting back to Howard's modest beginnings. He lived in a Levittown-type split-level house and was perfectly happy in middle-class suburbia. When Howard was ten years old, he got his first tape recorder, and soon after that started a band known as the Plumbers Union. The band subsequently changed its name to the Electric Comic Book. If you were lucky enough to catch the "This Is a Life?" episode of the old WWOR-TV show, you could have seen the much-awaited reunion of The Electric Comic Book performing their hit single, "Psychodelic Bee."

When Howard entered junior high, blacks began to move into his Roosevelt, Long Island, neighborhood. Howard contends that this triggered a mass exodus of anyone who was without color—except, of course, the Sterns. You see, Ben and Ray, especially Ray, believed that all people could get along with each other and that all races could live together in harmony.

However, while Ray was making friends with her new neighbors, Howard was beginning to understand what it felt like to be a minority in his own school—although, according to his old gym teacher, Mr. Chestnut, Howard was far from the only white kid at Roosevelt Junior High. In fact, the ratio of blacks to whites was probably in the three-to-two range.

Even so, Howard was now a tall, skinny Jewish kid (or is he "half-Jewish," as he contends?) in a predominantly black junior high school, and he stood out quite obviously from the rest of the crowd. He was often a target for the thugs in the school, who happened to be black. On an episode of the *Howard Stern Show*, Howard's parents told of an incident in which a young "Howdrie" or "Howchie," (nicknames Howard's parents still refer to him by) had a garbage pail thrown at his head. Howard has stated that it was his sense of humor that helped him survive those trying years.

Some folks in the media believe Howard's last years in Roosevelt have left him with a lot of negative feelings toward blacks. They cite such examples as the time Howard told the Pointer Sisters that he wanted to be their "Massa Howard." They forget to mention that the Pointer Sisters have a great sense of humor and laughed when he said it. The critics also point out the fact that Howard often refers to Hempstead, Long Island, as Hempstead, Africa. They fail to mention that Howard repeatedly had as a guest on his TV show a member of the Ku Klux Klan, and every time the Klan member appeared Howard was able to expose the man's complete ignorance of blacks and all other ethnic groups, and to render his prejudices meaningless.

No, I don't think Howard is a racist. I think he has opinions about race, but that does not necessarily make someone a racist. I also think that a white person can make jokes about black people without being a racist. Has anyone ever heard Eddie Murphy's comedy routines? How come I never hear Murphy referred to as a racist? I don't believe he is, much as I don't believe Howard is. I also don't believe too many people would choose a black woman as their broadcasting partner for over a decade if they were racist.

Back to the history. By the time Howard turned fifteen, his parents moved to a predominantly Irish Catholic and Protestant neighborhood. The move to Rockville Centre, Long Island, happened about the time that Howard was entering high school. I guess if Howard's experiences in Roosevelt colored his opinions about blacks, as the media would have us believe, then his time in Rockville Centre must have done the same for him in regards to Catholics.

HOWARD'S FIRST RADIO GIG, HOWARD'S FIRST FIRING

Along with three friends, Howard created a student radio show called *The King Schmaltz Bagel Hour*, which was a take-off on the old *King Biscuit Flour Hour*. It was during this time that Howard got to try out the style of radio that would endear him to millions of fans many years later.

This period holds the honored distinction of having been the first time that Howard was thrown off the air. The bit that got him bounced was a skit called "Godzilla Goes to Harlem." In it, the giant green monster descends on Harlem to wreak havoc, much like he had been doing to the Japanese for years. Unfortunately for the big-screen reptile, he ends up getting mugged by a couple of black guys.

As a matter of fact, he later was suspended from his job at WNBC-AM in New York for a skit called "Virgin Mary Kong," sometimes described as God's video game, in which men chase Mary around tables at a singles bar. The enlightened readers of this book will have realized by now that Howard Stern is not prejudiced. Howard would be prejudiced if he singled out blacks or Catholics or gays or Jews to joke about, but he does not.

A self-professed "equal opportunity offender," Howard is one of the fairest guys around because he picks on everybody and everything, including himself—*primarily* himself. The real prejudice lies with the executives at WNBC who suspended Howard over "Virgin Mary Kong," but arguably would not have done the same thing if the skit had been "Buddha Mario Bros." or "Allah Pac-Man."

Howard was an average high school student. He reportedly scored a total of 1,200 on his math and verbal SATs, which allowed him to be accepted at Boston University. "I heard it was an excellent place to pick up women," Howard has been quoted as saying. Howard majored in communications at BU, and it was there that he got his start in radio.

Not all the memories of his time at Boston University were bad ones, because this was where he met his future wife, Alison. One of Howard's proudest accomplishments is having met and married his extremely attractive wife before he became famous. Alison, from Newton, Massachusetts, must have been looking for a guy with a good sense of humor, because Howard was no Mel Gibson; he was more like a 6 foot, 4 inch Henry Gibson with a large nose. Sorry, Howard. I do think your look has improved since your early years but, hey, you can't have everything.

Anyway, Alison has got to be a saint of a woman to put up with all that Howard dishes her way. The most famous of these incidents (and the most troubling to the press) was the time when Howard joked about a miscarriage his wife had recently experienced. "I went on and joked about how I took pictures of the miscarriage from the toilet seat and sent them to her parents because they wanted pictures of their grandchildren. Alison flipped out," recalled Howard. I think Howard might admit that he went too far that day; I'm sure he had to do his penance at home for quite some time.

Another favorite prank of Howard's is to tell the most gorgeous of his guests, such as Belinda Carlisle or Alyssa Milano, that his wife either (a) just perished in a car accident or (b) has breast cancer and has told him he can start dating. At times, they almost believe him. Alison also has to listen to her husband spanking various bimbettes, put up with the babes who want Howard to paint their breasts green for St. Patrick's Day, and endure the aural excitement of Howard getting a rubdown.

Alison must dread it when the phone rings at home in the morning and Howard is on the other end wanting to discuss on the air why she would not "put out" for him the night before. If Alison ever decides she wants to end the marriage, Howard wouldn't stand a chance at the divorce proceedings. All this stuff is on tape!

In reality, the joking masks the fact that Howard is a truly devoted father and husband. After his radio show goes off the air and he finishes up at the office, he returns to his family on Long Island—wife Alison and their three young children, Emily, Debra, and baby, Ashley Jade. Howard doesn't smoke, drink, or take drugs anymore. He claims he experimented with a variety of drugs while in college, but what college student in the early '70s didn't? Let's face it, now that we have a president who openly admitted that he smoked pot, inhale or no inhale, the fact that Howard experimented with drugs should not be terribly disturbing to anyone. (Except to New York's Drug Enforcement Administration, who took seriously a humorous on-air reference to drug taking and led Howard to seek legal counsel.)

In 1976, Howard received his diploma from Boston University and began working at WRNW-FM. WRNW was a small, 3,000-watt rock station located in Briarcliff Manor, New

HOWARD AND THE DRUG ENFORCEMENT ADMINISTRATION

Howard's troubles with the government have not always been limited to the FCC. In 1988, Howard joked on air about having to supply drugs to some of his guests during his pay-per-view special, "Howard Stern's Underpants and Negligee Party." A DEA agent, who apparently did not get the joke, wrote a letter to the *New York Daily News* condemning Mr. Stern for his boasting about being a drug supplier.

Even though Howard was publicly miffed by the letter, nothing ever came of the incident, except that Howard received a severe scolding from his mother. "Howard, you kid around about these drugs, and people take you for real," Ray told him on the air. Howard explained that there was absolutely no substance to the allegations, but Ray thought all the problems could have been avoided if she had been at the party. Although I'm not sure Howard wanted the world to see his mother in her underpants.

York. Howard worked as a disc jockey, production director, and program director, earning a whopping $96 dollars a week. Ironically, another disc jockey who was getting her start at the same station at the same time was Meg Griffin, who now is at K-Rock with Howard and is often the brunt of Howard's piercing humor. Howard's stay at WRNW lasted two years, even though he was told by the station manager to "shut up and just play music" for the housewives. It was from this point that Howard began his real journey, straight to the big time.

CHAPTER 2

STATION CHANGES

n 1978, Howard was offered a job for $12,000 per year as the "Morning Man" at WCCC AM-FM in Hartford, Connecticut. Howard was able to convince the station's owner that mixing listener phone calls with the music was a good idea. Anybody who was listening, those many years ago, will tell you that this early show was both more political and more serious than Howard's radio shows today.

The Hartford show was a good experience for Howard, and it led him to an important discovery: "Frightening" Fred Norris, or Fred "Earth Dog" Norris (take your pick of nicknames, he's been labeled both). A college student working at WCCC when Howard discovered him, Fred quickly signed up as the first member of Stern's backup group.

Nowadays, Fred plays Kurt Waldheim Jr., a recurring on-air character who loves to have contestants play "Guess Who's the Jew." He is also "Mr. Blackswell," the other half of "Out of the Closet Stern." He does many of the voice-overs for the various bits, does vocals on song parodies, writes material, feeds Howard lines, makes sure the commercials get aired during the radio show, accompanies all the zany proceedings with some creative and deftly placed sound effects, and can even accompany a visiting musician on the guitar if need be. Fred will do practically anything for the show, including proposing to "Princess Norris," a girl he met on "Dial-a-Date," while on the air. But he won't let Howard go in his precious "Bug" or visit his apartment.

Fred, like anyone else, must take his lumps from Howard. Howard had two days' worth of material when he found out that Fred's gift to his mom for Mother's Day was a Carvel "Cookie Puss" cake. Howard had a field day as he made fun of Fred's choice of gifts. "Hey, mom, this year I got you a Slurpee," Howard mocked. Fred's uncircumcised manliness has also been the subject of many spirited discussions on the show. Last I heard, Fred had his own fan club, and he's deserving of it. Fred, we're glad Howard happened across you!

In two years, Howard's popularity at the Hartford station soared, and so did the ratings. However, in 1980, Howard was offered $50,000 a year to move to Detroit. "You got a better offer, you go," Howard explained. Unfortunately, Howard was unable to bring Fred along with him, but it didn't really matter, as Howard was not destined to stay there long; he worked for nine months as the morning man for WWWW, known as W4, before the station decided to go country on him. For Howard, it was obvious that this was not going to be his home. As he told *New York Magazine*, "I have no tolerance for country music. I mean, the Judds remind me of Nazi women. I feel they would kill me."

The amazing thing about Howard's brief stay in Detroit was that it was the first and only time that he has ever been honored by his own industry. Howard was actually named *Billboard* magazine's top album-oriented rock personality for 1980. This recognition most likely helped him land his next job—at WWDC-FM (DC-101) in the nation's capital.

It was at DC-101 that Howard developed into the radio genius we know and love today. It was also the place where he met an ex–air force nurse named Robin Quivers, who was working at DC-101 as a serious news reporter. Robin, who is a few years older than Howard, began her career with Howard as a "professional newsperson" who would come on near the end of his show to discuss the latest happenings in Washington and around the country. Much like they do today, Robin would deliver the news from a different studio while Howard would make commentary and crack jokes. He would also needle Quivers relentlessly about her sex life.

The chemistry was so strong between the two that Robin became a permanent part of the show, and now serves as his cohost. To this day, Robin still sits in a different room during the broadcasts that you hear in the morning. It's hard to know why. Is it superstition, or the fact that Howard claims to be protecting her from the gas he frequently passes?

Robin has been called an "irritating woman," a "laugh track," a "straight man," and a "sidekick" by the press. One thing she certainly is is an integral part of the entire Howard Stern empire, including radio, TV, and videos. Back in 1981, Howard told the *Washington Post* that [Robin] "transcends being a newsperson; she has a personality in her own right. She's uninhibited, says what's on her mind." Howard has since updated his praise for Robin, stating, "There is no better on-air partner." If Howard's the King of Media, Robin is the Queen.

No longer just the "news reporter" on Howard's show, she is also a great interviewer in her own right, and let's not forget that she plays Ray to Howard's Bob on their version of the great radio team of Bob and Ray. In one skit, Bob did a reading of his poem "Kill, Kill, Kill the Hippies" and insisted that poetry is not "homo stuff." Ray (Robin, in a he-manized voice) responded, "There was some real men who once upon a time wrote poetry, but the homos took it over."

Robin who made her TV sitcom debut with a guest role on *Fresh Prince of Bel-Air* in November 1993, can also stand on her own two feet when it comes to handling Howard's type of humor. One day, a female listener called up and told Howard that she was in bed with her husband. Howard told them that if they would make love while he listened over the phone, he would send them Joe Jackson tickets. After a lot of panting and moaning, Howard observed, "I smell Joe Jackson tickets." Robin, showing the kind of quick wit usually associated with her partner, replied, "Is that what you smell?"

Give a listen to the show sometime, focusing on Robin's contribution. You'll be surprised how funny she is in her own right. Let's face it, Robin is important to the show in one other respect—she is a black female. Obviously, this should not matter at all, and I don't think it matters to anyone but the people who constantly attack Howard as a racist and a chauvinist. I think the extremely intelligent Robin Quivers shows everyone that you don't need to get offended over every little joke directed at your particular minority. Regular guest Young MC, the rap star, has been quoted as saying that he thinks Howard is funny but that "sometimes he goes too far on the black jokes." Funny how Young MC doesn't think he goes too far on the Jewish or gay jokes. Robin, on the other hand, has made it clear that Howard's racial humor does not bother her. Only once in a blue moon will Howard and Robin argue. And Robin usually prevails.

Most fans of the Stern show could not care less about Robin's race, but they do love the fact that she is very attractive, with breasts that are "thick and juicy," to quote Howard. Her luscious love lumps are a size 36D, down from a double D after a 1990 reduction operation. Robin realizes that to be on the Stern show you must be able to poke fun at yourself as well as

Robin: Nice hair! (Fred Blake/Star File)

everyone else. Robin, an admitted "three input" woman, once
sang a version of "Strangers in the Night" that contained lines
like, "I won't spread my legs unless your name is Sting" and
"My hooters big and ripe" are like a "plushy Disneyland."

While they were in Washington, Howard and Robin
became so popular the station allowed Howard to track down
his old friend Fred Norris, "King of Mars" (nickname number
three), and bring him to Washington as Howard's producer. The
three of them teamed up to nearly triple the ratings at DC-101.
They did it with their particular brand of humor, the type that
people were not used to hearing on their radios: weather
reports from "God," "Born-Again Stern," and the newly developed "Out of the Closet Stern," the gay character which Howard
continues to perform to this day.

According to the *Washington Post*, other bits that Howard
created during his first stay in Washington included Dial-a-
Date (Gay Dial-a-Date, Impressionist Dial-a-Date, Dwarf Dial-a-
Date, etc.), cash giveaways that amounted to whatever Howard

Howard and Robin in Los Angeles. (Jeffrey Mayer/Star File)

had in pocket change, and "Beaver breaks." These were radio sketches in which the Cleaver family dealt with such topics as Wally and his inflatible rubber doll and Ward's decision about whether or not to have a sex change operation.

Howard was so controversial that DC-101 was forced to install a seven-second delay—not to control the callers, but to contain Howard himself. One of Howard's funniest and most controversial moments while he was in Washington took place after Air Florida's flight number 90 had plunged into the Potomac in 1982. Howard decided to call the airline to ask what its one-way fare was from the National Airport to the 14th Street Bridge.

Although Howard's popularity soared during his stay in Washington, he was not very happy with the station. Howard has mentioned on the air that he detested station manager Goff Lebhar, whom he makes fun of to this day. Howard felt that

Lebhar underappreciated him, "making me appear at high schools and shit." It was for this reason, along with the need to make the "Big Time," that Howard jumped at the chance to move to New York and join WNBC. Howard ended up being officially fired from DC-101, but only after he had signed the contract with WNBC and only weeks before his contract expired at the Washington radio station.

WNBC was definitely the Big Time. A 50,000-watt AM station, it was already the home of Don Imus and Soupy Sales. Howard was allowed to bring Robin and Fred with him, and the move also allowed him to move back home to Long Island. Howard was given the afternoon "drive time" slot, and was paid a nice salary of $200,000 dollars a year. It was 1982, and Howard was twenty-eight years old and broadcasting on one of the most powerful stations in the most happening city in the world. It seemed that things couldn't get much better—but, as Howard found out pretty quickly, they could get much worse.

Right from the start, WNBC's management had trouble with Howard Stern's act. It was as if they had never listened to the guy when he was in Washington. I think it is fair to say at this point that WNBC had to be one of the worst-managed radio stations in history. They were even worse judges of talent. As mentioned earlier, in his first year at WNBC, Howard was suspended for "Virgin Mary Kong." He began to feud with the Morning Man, Don Imus, as well as fellow broadcaster Soupy Sales. To top it off, his ratings were not soaring like they had in Washington, Detroit, or Hartford. In his second year at WNBC, he was in seventh place in the afternoon time slot.

Surprisingly, the ratings were weak despite such bits as "Hillel Street Blues," a Jewish cop drama, and the song "The Twelve Days of Martial Law," which attacked the Polish government and contained the following lyrics: "My government took from me—five nasal hair clippers, four orders of pig feet, three green bowling shirts . . . " Howard would constantly draw the ire of WNBC executives with lines like "It wasn't the Jews who killed Jesus; I have a strong suspicion that it was two

Howard and Fred Norris and the FCC rally at Dag Hammarskjöld Plaza, 1987.
(Chuck Pulin/Star File)

Puerto Rican guys." He would also get himself into trouble with his live commercials, such as the one for a New York furrier in which he talked about skinning cats for a jacket while Fred played a tape of squealing kittens in the background. Neither the furrier nor management was pleased with the ad-libs that Howard included in his rendition of the fur commercial.

Nevertheless, some good things *did* happen at WNBC. First of all, certain celebrities started noticing Howard's talent. Eddie Murphy, Steve Allen, and future good friend Joan Rivers, among others, began to make appearances on his show. And, it was at this station that he began working with writer Al Rosenberg and a young intern named Gary Dell'Abate. "Boy" Gary has gone on to become not only Howard's producer, but also his public whipping boy for the past ten years.

Although Howard picks on everyone, especially those he works with, his favorite target of all time would have to be Boy Gary. As any frequent listener to the radio show will tell you, Gary brings a lot of this upon himself. The most famous incident involving Gary was the one that earned him his second nickname, "Baba Booey." Gary started collecting animation cells, which are original cartoon drawings. One day on the air, Howard decided to begin busting him for this new hobby, which was a rather expensive one. Gary, trying to defend himself, decided to talk about how fast the art appreciates in value and cited the example of a Quick-Draw McGraw and "Baba Booey" piece. Even though Howard missed it the first time Gary said it, Gary, like a person who seems to seek out abuse, decided to repeat "Baba Booey."

Well, as anyone who knows old Huckleberry Hound cartoons can tell you, the character's name is Baba Looey. Howard did not let him get away with making the same mistake twice. Here is a man spending thousands of dollars on cartoon paintings and he doesn't even know the name of the characters he's buying. Howard not only jumped on him for this, but began playing the tape-recorded voice of Gary saying "Baba Booey" every time Gary entered the studio. This soon led to a string of phony phone calls to the office, in which Gary thought he was talking to job applicants or old friends, only to have the caller eventually get in a "Baba Booey" reference and piss Gary off something fierce.

My favorite was when Gary had finally had enough of the phone calls and had someone else answer the phone. The caller, played by Billy West, asked to speak to Gary and told the female assistant that it was "Barbara." Gary, who has an aunt named Barbara, got on the phone, thinking that he was finally receiving a legitimate call. When Gary finally realized that it was not the Barbara he thought it was, he asked, "Who is this?" The caller answered, "Barbara Booey." Click. He had been had once again.

Gary is also known for his teeth, which are unusually big. Howard has often talked about Gary's "horse teeth" and their "green glow." He tried to send Gary to his dentist on a number of occasions. On the TV show, Gary had to wear different masks for the first few weeks to hide his distracting teeth from the camera. He played Toothy on "Pee Wee's Play With Yourself House," and he wore a helmet with an attached personal irrigation spraying system for his teeth and gums on one of the episodes.

Finally, in what has to be classified as one of the most disgusting moments ever filmed, Gary ate simulated shit from a baby's diaper as the gorilla in "Jungleman," a skit on Howard's "Butt Bongo Fiesta." ("It's still warm, too. Good job, you little bastid!")

Although Gary is constantly getting publicly berated by Howard, he must be doing something right, as Howard threatens but never fires the "Boy" producer. And why should he—it can't be the easiest job in the world to line up guests for the radio show, and Howard has had on some of the best. Conversely, Gary knows that the Stern show is the place to be. He has stated, "I'd rather be a moron on the *Howard Stern Show* than be a star on Imus or WNEW."

Now, let's go back to WNBC and 1984. The ratings began to go up that year, but his feuds with management, and his relations with the other jocks, grew worse. Howard was getting frustrated with everything about WNBC, he was tired of playing records, and he thought the other jocks were a "bunch of no-talents." Howard especially detested program director Kevin Metheny, whom he nicknamed "Pig Virus."

Things deteriorated to the point that Howard got into an on-air shoving match with John Hayes, WNBC's general manager. Finally, in September of 1985, the ax fell, despite the fact that Howard had just received the highest ratings ever. He had succeeded in taking his time slot from number eleven, where it had started out, to number one. Yet he was fired from a station that had Don Imus working for it. Don Imus is just as offensive as Howard; he just isn't funny.

Howard thinks he knows why he was fired. He told *Rolling Stone* magazine, "The story goes that Thornton Bradshaw, the chairman of the board of RCA [NBC's then-parent company], was riding in his limo one day, and he turned on the station

THE BOY GARY IMPERSONATOR

Well, they
say that imitation is the
sincerest form of flattery, but I'm
not sure that holds true in this case.
Gary had a man impersonating him who
would call up unsuspecting females and tell
them that they would win $50,000 in a "Howard
Stern Show"-sponsored contest if they met the
impostor at a specified location while wearing a
miniskirt without panties. At one point, the police
had received thirty-two complaints about the
"fake Baba Booey." Apparently, the impostor was
having some success, as one victim told
Howard how her husband had given the fake
Gary the names and phone numbers of
women friends who might be willing to
participate in the contest. Hey, no
one's claimed that all of
Howard's listeners are
brain surgeons.

and heard me talking about doing 'Bestiality Dial-a-Date.' And I guess he didn't think it was too fucking funny."

According to the book *Three Blind Mice*, a national best-seller about the downfall of network TV, Howard was actually terminated because of Grant Tinker, NBC chairman, who the book says did not like Stern's brand of humor. An NBC employee is reported to have been told by Tinker, "Look, if that's the only way to make money we shouldn't be in the business." Well, in at least one respect, Mr. Tinker was correct: NBC soon left the New York radio scene.

Firing Howard may have been the biggest mistake NBC has ever made. Bigger than "Hello, Larry" or losing David Letterman. Howard was quoted in *New York Magazine* as stating, "We took an unhip radio station and completely changed it. . . . For three years, we prevented the dinosaur from dying." After Howard was fired, the radio station started its long slide into oblivion. Once Howard targeted Don Imus and morning radio in New York, it was only a matter of time before WNBC became WFAN and went to an all-sports format. Eventually, the old WNBC station was bought by Howard's next employer, Infinity Broadcasting.

Let's think about this for just a second. One man was responsible for bringing down a broadcasting giant like WNBC: Howard Stern. What about all the executives at NBC who had Howard under contract and decided to let him go, only to have him to go out and destroy their radio station? Exactly how stupid can a company get? The top brass decided to let go of their bright, young, hilarious, star, who was no more offensive than their washed-up, over-the-hill, loser of a Morning Man. John P. Hayes Jr., WNBC's vice president and general manager, blamed the firing on "conceptual differences"; he should have blamed it on pure stupidity at RCA, NBC, and WNBC—stupidity that must still haunt them on a daily basis, especially between 6 and 10:30 A.M. every weekday. The irony is that Howard and Imus now collect a paycheck from the same company, Infinity Broadcasting.

3
CHAPTER

HOWARD
STERN
ALL
MORNING

Almost immediately after Howard was fired from WNBC in September 1985, radio stations from around the country started calling him with offers. One California radio station offered both radio and TV, but Stern was determined to stay in New York. "I want to kick NBC's ass," Stern was quoted as saying. After a very brief stint on the comedy club circuit around New York and New Jersey, Howard was made an offer by Infinity Broadcasting president Mel Karmazin. On November 18, 1985, Howard was back on the air, at WXRK, otherwise known as K-Rock, as its afternoon man. He brought with him Robin, Fred, and Gary.

After four months, Howard was moved to the morning time slot, replacing Jay Thomas, to do battle with his old rival, Don Imus. Imus proved to be no challenge at all, as Howard took a new, struggling FM station and boosted it within the year from number twenty-one in the ratings to number one. When he passed WNBC in the morning ratings, he staged his first of many mock funerals for defeated rival stations, this one outside the corporate offices at Rockefeller Center. "Imus said if we ever beat him, he'd eat a dead dog's dick," Howard told *Rolling Stone*. "And I was going to send him one, but I felt bad for the dog."

After moving into first place among all morning shows, Howard staged a mobile victory parade in which Howard and crew were driven around Manhattan, along with an outdoor press conference in Times Square. Howard and the crew were shouting through loudspeakers that Howard was the King of New York radio. At the press conference, Howard stated, "As I look at you, I see a sea of losers like me. Who would ever think that a sea of losers like you would make a loser like me number one?"

The teaming of Howard and K-Rock was a match made in heaven. Management was, and is, willing to back Howard up, and rarely feuds with Howard over his distinctive style. "This is the best place I've ever worked," says Howard. To make things even better, K-Rock allowed Howard to rehire a second writer, a stand-up comedian by the name of Jackie "the Joke Man" Martling, who had joined the Stern team at the end of the NBC run.

Jackie was the runner-up to Steve O., a mediocre comedian, on the comedy portion of *Star Search*, the talent show hosted by "that big load," according to Howard, Ed McMahon.

Jackie was a comic from Long Island, whose act consisted of telling the type of jokes you would hear in a men's locker room; he is not very funny, in my personal opinion. He had a stint hosting a comedy show, *Spotlight Cafe*, which was on directly after *The Howard Stern Show* on WOR-TV in New York, and the show was a bomb. Jackie is at his best when feeding

Howard, Robin, Jackie, and Fred in Los Angeles, 1992. (Fred Blake/Star File)

lines to Howard on his radio show. He is also the person laughing raucously in the background during the radio show.

On many occasions this laughter has come back to haunt Jackie. Fred will play a tape of Jackie's guffaw after a particularly sad news story, thus making Jackie look insensitive. And in one show, Jackie's laugh was ridiculed by the whole gang, and compared, appropriately, to the sound of a whistling train.

The problem with Jackie is that he seems to think that he is too talented to be in the background. He has gotten a bit better about this, but it was only a couple of years ago that he actually left the show for a day or two over a contract dispute with WXRK's management. Howard wished him well, but Jackie was back in the nest soon after.

Howard has had plenty of opportunity to pick on Jackie. Jackie at one time before doing stand-up, thought he had a career in country music. Jackie's song "Flies" is a hoot. Howard had a field day with that song, among others we've heard played on the show, including "The Pot Song." Many of these songs sound like a cross between *Deliverance* and the "Beer

Barrel Polka." The funniest thing about Jackie's music career is
that he thinks he has a lot of talent, when it is pretty obvious to
Howard and everyone else listening that he doesn't.

Jackie also has some physical deformities, which Howard
often brings to the attention of his television viewers. Due to a
poor diet (according to Howard) Jackie has some really ugly rot-
ted toenails that he decided to have removed. Howard, never
missing an opportunity for a unique viewing experience, decided to film the operation for his TV show. I have never seen anything that looked as painful as the doctor ripping Jackie's toenails out, one by one. Pitifully, after the operation was over,
Jackie's toes looked even worse than they had before the operation.

Jackie also loves to show off his protruding stomach and
belly button. On the TV show, we saw him in a state of undress
doing a fantastic impression of a pregnant Demi Moore in her
Vanity Fair cover pose. For the Pee Wee Herman parody, Jackie
painted his belly and played "Globey." Although I feel Jackie
thinks a little too much of himself, he definitely adds to the proceedings, and I hope he decides to stick around.

Howard's popularity in New York seems to know no limits.
He is now at least a football field ahead of his closest competitor in New York, which is an all-news radio station.

After hitting the hay at 8 P.M.. and masturbating himself to
sleep, Howard gets up before the sun. "Ronnie the Limo Driver"
picks Howard up around 5 A.M. at his Long Island home for the
half-hour drive into Manhattan, during which time Howard
meditates. (He's an avid believer in transcendental meditation.)
From 5:30 until showtime at 6 A.M., Howard searches the local
papers, plus the mailbag and the fax machine, for material to
use on the show. Just before going on the air, he enters the studio and puts on his headphones. Then he proceeds to put out
the funniest and most entertaining radio show in history.

If there is anyone out there who is living in some sort of
vacuum and does not know the format of the *Howard Stern
Show*, it is quite simply the following:

1● There is an opening sequence of material that has been prerecorded, from song parodies to talk show hosts discussing Stern to news events.

2● David Letterman "introduces" the "lovely and talented" Howard Stern, a snippet taken from one of Howard's many Letterman appearances, or some other introduction is made, such as Arsenio's from the time Howard made a memorable appearance on his show.

3● Starting about 6:15, Howard and Robin banter, which can be about anything. If something exciting has happened in the past twenty hours, you can be assured that it will be the first thing they talk about.

From this point on, the rest of the show is a real crapshoot. Any of the following things could happen:

1● Howard could talk about gays. "I had a friend who was gay; his father kicked the crap out of him. You should have seen him. (Now) he porks girls like you wouldn't believe."

2● Howard could talk about his sex life. "The closest I came to making love to a black woman was when I masturbated to a picture of Aunt Jemima."

3● He could interview celebrities either in the studio or over the phone. These can range from Milton Berle to Joe Walsh to Jessica Hahn to Joey Buttafuoco. Anybody who is anybody has been interviewed by Howard—unless, of course, he or she is scared of Howard. Frankly, that does include quite a chunk of the celebrity population. (Most reluctant celebrities who finally do appear on the show are pleasantly surprised to find that they enjoy the experience.)

4● Howard will talk about celebrities who won't come on his show. "She's the Big Fat Blob" and "He's the Ricky Ricardo of the nineties," he's stated about Roseanne and Tom Arnold.

5● He'll play a song parody. One, to the tune of "Do You Believe in Magic," was a ditty about Magic Johnson. It contained the line, "Oh that Magic, when he banged you good, he didn't wear rubbers though he knew that he should . . . "

6● He could talk about his own political ideology. "Any woman who votes for George Bush might as well put her vagina in an envelope and mail it to the White House," he stated when talking about abortion.

7● Howard could transform himself into one of his on-air personalities, such as Elvis (who supposedly loved "the lump of fat on my mama's neck"), Ted and Joan Kennedy, "Out of the Closet Stern," Bob of "Bob and Ray," or a host of other characters.

8● You could hear one of his specialty shows, such as the Christmas or birthday shows, or his live broadcasts from the Grammys or from London.

9● You could hear one of his "Phony Phone Calls." On one occasion, in one of the funniest conversations ever recorded, Howard called the London Medical College in order to place a bid on the remains of the Elephant Man. There ensued a real conversation between Howard and a British nurse. Howard began by explaining the purpose of his call, and added temptingly, "I know that Michael Jackson offered a million and Lisa Lisa offered a million and a half; I can up that to two million." But he met with immediate rejection. Unwilling to take no for an answer, Howard tried to reason with the nurse. "All I really want is like a leg or an arm or the hump," he pleaded. The nurse sensed that Howard might be pulling her leg, but he assured her of his sincerity and pressed on. Another rejection followed. Howard then lowered his sights and asked, "Do you have any other remains that are ugly?" The nurse was appalled. "That . . . that . . . that is *sick!!*" she exclaimed. Howard apologized. "It's not that I mean to be sick," he explained,

HOWARD STERN'S TOP TEN SONG PARODIES

-1-
"Don't You Dare Have
Lunch With Jeffrey Dahmer" (sung
by Peter Noone to the tune of "Mrs.
Brown, You've Got a Lovely Daughter")

-2-
"Cancer Man" (sung in Sammy Davis Jr.
voice to the tune of "Candy Man")

-3-
"Angry Young Meg" (sung to the tune of "Angry Young
Man"; a homage to Meg Griffin)

-4-
"Sounds of Kinison" (touching tribute song sung to the tune of
"Sounds of Silence")

-5-
"Breasts Feed the World" (star-studded benefit song sung to the
tune of "We Are the World")

-6-
"Baldy, Baldy" (pays homage to the Philadelphia Zoo Keep-er,
whose unofficial theme song had been "Louie, Louie")

-7-
"Howard Stern Xmas Song" (sung by spokesmodels on the
WWOR-TV show to the tune of "Jingle Bells." Contained the classic line, "Howard Stern, Howard Stern, he is number one; he's so
funny, he's so cute, he makes our juices run")

-8-
"Dear Chevy" (spoof of "Dear Jesus" at the expense of Chevy
Chase)

-9-
"Ted the Janitor" (tribute song sung with feeling by
Fred Norris to the tune of "Desperado")

-10-
"Roll Him" (musical jab directed at a
favorite target, Regis Philbin.
Sung to "Proud Mary"
and about Regis's
"flipper-footed
son")

adding that he merely wanted "any weird remains—Skunk Girl or a Sheep Boy, anything that's weird . . . Chicken Girl . . ." The nurse had heard enough and hung up and Howard and the gang cracked up. Jeez, I can't understand why the British are always calling us "ugly Americans."

10● Howard could be throwing a funeral for a newly conquered rival disc jockey.

11● He could be talking to one of his family members. "Honey, could you give birth today? I would like a three-day weekend," he once stated to his very pregnant wife.

12● He could be taking listener phone calls, which he often does by spinning a wheel because of all the cities he is currently heard in.

13● You could hear one of the prerecorded parodies of such TV classics as *Lost in Space*, *I Love Lucy*, or *Mayberry R.F.D.* One Mayberry bit had Floyd the Barber as a cocaine dealer and Aunt Bee being gang-banged by a bunch of bikers. "They're forcing me to act out double penetration" and "Bring me another stud biker" are just two of the lines Aunt Bee, played by Howard himself, has in this tribute to the old sitcom classic. I think Howard was trying to point out that Mayberry has changed with the times, just like everything else.

14● Or how about such movie classics as "Buttman" and "My Gay Left Foot" both of which starred "Out of the Closet Stern." There was also "A Christmas Carol," with Fred the Elephant Boy as the "Ghost of Speech Impediment Past" and "Quentin the Stutterer" as Scrooge.

15● Of course, you could always get lucky and catch one of the many "Dial-a-Date" shows. I think "Lesbian Dial-a-Date" is everyone's favorite, but each one is funny in its own special way.

16● You could hear real politicians calling in and campaigning on Howard's show. What political strategist possessed the genius to have Jerry Brown call Howard while making a run at the presidency in 1992? (Howard believed in Brown and backed him, until Brown ignored him and Howard moved his allegiance to Bill Clinton.)

17● Then, of course, there is the news. This is when Robin reverts back to her old job of being a news reporter and comments on the previous day's occurrences. Howard is like a color commentator as he adds his own perspective to each story. For example, Robin reported that Amy Fisher was spotted at a Cher concert, where she talked to her attorney and "played with her hair." Howard: "Which hair—the hair in her shorts?" Another time, Robin reported on the fact that Boris Yeltsin had asked the United States for economic support. Howard: "Those stupid, lazy bastard Russians. They're under communism so long they can't even produce anything."

Or . . . Robin: "Audrey Hepburn had a malignant tumor removed from her colon." Stern: "Can I buy it? That's memorabilia."

Or . . . Robin: "The navy has decided to reinstate a gay officer." Howard: "When I get nude in front of a gay guy, they get so hot that they can't control themselves."

18● Then again, you may have the pleasure of hearing Howard berate a female from his past. Karen was a teenage "friend" of Howard's. After coaxing her into admitting that she had never looked upon him "as a guy," Howard launched into a tirade. "Man, that's why I make women suffer every day on this show . . . bitches . . . all of you with your sex, like it's golden."

19● Or you could hear the world's greatest rock musicians play their classic music live in order to please Howard. It is pretty amazing how much the rock world loves Howard, as

THE CASTAWAYS FROM HELL

Another favorite radio parody was a *Gilligan's Island* takeoff which Howard did after the disappearance of media mogul Robert Maxwell. In this one, the billionaire Maxwell washed up onto the island inhabited by the castaways right after "Hairyann" (played by Gary) had given birth to Gilligan's child. The castaways, who obviously had run out of coconuts, proceeded to eat the baby. "Mrs. Bowel" (played by Jackie) stated, "I never thought that I'd ever like placenta." Robert Maxwell must have looked like one large filet mignon to the castaways as the Skipper said, "Well, little buddy, it's been three days since we devoured Robert Maxwell." Gilligan replied, "Yeah, and I had a ball." The Skipper finished the bit with "Yeah, and I had the other one."

HOWARD AND THE NEW JERSEY TURNPIKE

Howard Stern has become a real player in the world of politics. He may have even decided the outcome of the 1993 New Jersey gubernatorial race between incumbent Democrat Jim Florio and dark-horse Republican challenger Christie Whitman.

In what can only be described as a brilliant political move by the challenger, Ms. Whitman went on the *Howard Stern Show* the day before the election and asked for Howard to throw his support her way. This strategy was so perfect, because it allowed her to gain the support of Stern fans but did not allow her opponent any time to attack her for making the appearance. Ms. Whitman ended up coming from behind in the polls to narrowly win the election.

In return for delivering the vote to Ms. Whitman, Howard only asked for one small favor: He just wants a rest stop on the New Jersey Turnpike to be named after him. Governor Whitman has promised to pursue the idea. Hell, if nothing else, at least name a bathroom stall at the Vince Lombardi rest area after Howie.

he doesn't even play their records. Of course, he does sell a lot of records for them if they appear live on his show. Howard is responsible for breaking out a lot of previously unknown groups, such as the Black Crowes. Ian Anderson of Jethro Tull, Steven Tyler and Aerosmith, Papa John Phillips of the Mamas and the Papas, Belinda Carlisle of the Go-Gos, and Meat Loaf, among countless others, have all made appearances on Howard's show. He is also personal friends with Joe Walsh of the Eagles, Leslie West of Mountain, Dee Snyder of Twisted Sister/Widow Maker, and he even had Elton John compose a special song about him and his "small penis."

200 You'll always hear Howard plugging something, whether it is his own videotapes, or Jackie's comedy club dates, or the DJ service run by Scott the Engineer, or tickets to the scheduled appearances of his guests. If he's not doing one of the above plugs, he is probably doing a live commercial for Dial-a-Mattress or Snapple iced tea. Smart advertisers realize that Howard has the most loyal audience on the radio. I had never heard of Snapple iced tea before hearing Howard talk about it on his show. Now, it's a huge success, sold everywhere. And I can't live without it; I love the stuff!

Howard also admits that he would sell anything to anyone, but he has on more than one occasion warned his audience to beware. "If I was a disc jockey in Germany, I would have sold ovens to Hitler," he once stated on the air.

Ken Stevens, the general manager of Infinity's Washington and Philadelphia Radio Stations, has called Howard "the best radio salesman who exists today." An advertising spot on the Stern show is not cheap, either. In New York, the rates on his show for ads are among the highest in the market. I know from listening to the show myself that the $2,000 fee a sponsor pays for a live ad is well worth the money. No one dares to change the dial during a live commercial; it can often end up being just as funny as the rest of the Stern show. It is quite simple: Stern sells more products because his listeners pay attention to every word he says, while the rest of the radio dial has listeners switching from one station to the next as soon as a commercial begins to play. Boy, wouldn't a Snapple iced tea taste good right now?

21● You could hear an in-studio contest. On one occasion, Robin was blindfolded and tried to identify Gary, Jackie, Fred, and Howard by the smell of their crotches. She was wrong each time. I think this game provided one thing—that Robin can't keep her nose out of other people's business.

22● You could hear Howard answering his mail over the air, sort of like David Letterman's "Viewer Mail." Howard's mail seems to be a bit more hostile than David's. Stern's letters often start out like "What a stupid Jew, you should have been aborted" or "Heil Hitler, you Jew bastard." Robin's mail is not much better. "I want to hear about niggers murdering each other," one admiring fan wrote. I think it's really great when big stars like David Letterman and Howard Stern take the time to respond to their fans.

Okay, I have given you twenty-two different possibilities of what you could hear when you tune in to listen to Howard and Company, but I could go on forever, because the options are literally limitless. Anything can happen on the *Howard Stern Show!* And it often does. Unfortunately, no one can listen for the entire four and a half to five hours every day, so important things do get missed. Fortunately, there is the "Best of Stern," which is played while Howard is on vacation.

Howard's relationship with management at WXRK in New York seems to be about as copacetic as any business relationship could be. Except for an occasional dressing-down of general manager Tom Chiusano (or is it "cheap-a-sano") or ex–program director Mark Chernoff (who moved to WFAN), the ride has been a smooth one. I think Infinity President Mel Karmazin, who reportedly earns $750,000 dollars a year, realizes that the best way for him to keep earning that kind of money is to support Howard in every way possible. Infinity has done this amazingly well, under some tough pressure from various groups trying to get Howard off the air.

Infinity showed its support for Howard in the best way by taking his show—which is based in New York—and seeing how it would do in other markets. First stop: the City of Brotherly Love, Philadelphia.

Howard and Robin in Los Angeles, 1992. (Vincent Zuffante/Star File)

CHAPTER 4:

PHILADELPHIA:

FREEDOM

FROM

BALDY

BALDY

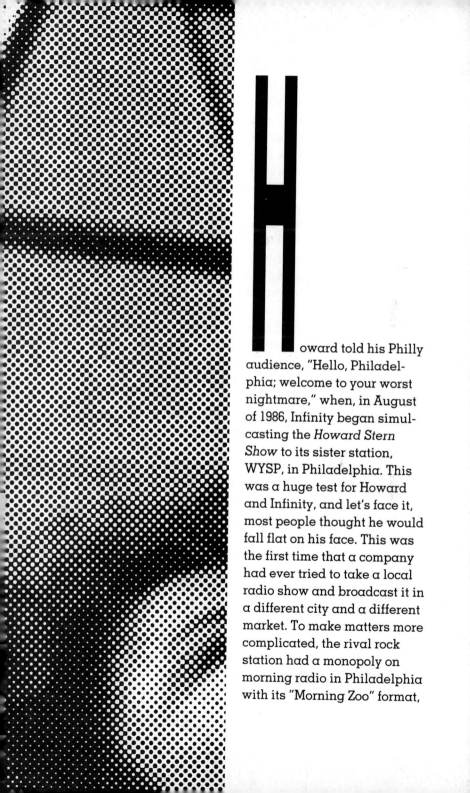

Howard told his Philly audience, "Hello, Philadelphia; welcome to your worst nightmare," when, in August of 1986, Infinity began simulcasting the *Howard Stern Show* to its sister station, WYSP, in Philadelphia. This was a huge test for Howard and Infinity, and let's face it, most people thought he would fall flat on his face. This was the first time that a company had ever tried to take a local radio show and broadcast it in a different city and a different market. To make matters more complicated, the rival rock station had a monopoly on morning radio in Philadelphia with its "Morning Zoo" format, hosted by that Legend in His Own Mind, John DeBella.

John DeBella was flying high with his Morning Zoo show on Philadelphia's WMMR radio station before Howard Stern came along. In 1986, his show had ratings as high as a 13 share, which is 13 percent of the listening audience, phenomenal by radio standards. The Morning Zoo format consisted of a couple of guys acting like ten-year-old children during the breaks between spinning Top Forty records. (The other ten-year-old in Philadelphia was Mark "the Shark" Drucker.) The format was not original to Philadelphia. Most of the time the credit—or blame—for this format has been placed at the feet of DJ Scott Shannon. This is the same Scott Shannon who used this format on a New York rock station before Howard chased him to the West Coast. Even the "inventor" of the Morning Zoo gave up the format, instead opting for an equally bad format called "Pirate Radio," which was subsequently taken off the air in Los Angeles.

In 1986 the options for radio listeners were very limited, and DeBella and his Morning Zoo reaped the benefits. Unfortunately for DeBella, he thought his run at the top would last forever, and he took every opportunity to rub people the wrong way. Rumors float about how DeBella thought so much of himself that he would not let WMMR interns make eye contact with him. DeBella reportedly once told a producer he was hiring, "Look, man, I am an absolute ass to work with."

Stern producer Gary Dell'Abate had the unenviable task of interning at a Long Island studio with John DeBella. Gary has often told how DeBella would not let an intern "look at him" or "talk to him." "He thought he was the highest talent in the world. . . . If you ever said anything to him, he would just glare at you right in the eye and not answer you."

This was the type of attitude typical of a guy whose show revolved around childish contests such as "diving for prizes in a trash Dumpster" and having stupid names for the days of the week: i.e., Monday Morning Blues, Double Shot Tuesday, Hump Day Wednesday, Thirsty Thursday, and Gonzo Friday. He is

STOP THAT WAKE

The infamous funeral took place directly outside WMMR studios, where DeBella was trying to concentrate on the zany antics of his Zoo. WMMR had attempted to have its legal counsel petition City Hall to stop the funeral, and according to *Philadelphia Magazine*, DeBella even offered $100 to a construction worker to use a jackhammer during it. Mark "the Shark" Drucker recalled, "We were a little subdued doing the Zoo that morning. It was like we were sitting around waiting for a hurricane."

Howard in Philadelphia to torture the Zoo Keeper, 1992. (Alex Lloyd Gross/ Star File)

also the guy who actually bragged, "Can WYSP do this with Howard Stern?" after his station sent the Zoo Keeper to serve coffee and doughnuts to people outside the Spectrum waiting for Paul McCartney tickets.

It was these kinds of "witty" stunts that were earning Mr. DeBella a base salary of a million dollars, along with ratings incentives to earn an extra $600,000 a year. When DeBella found out that Howard would be joining him on the Philadelphia airwaves, he stated, "Stern thinks I'll shake and quake in my boots, but I don't lose."

In another interview, DeBella really set himself up for the eventual Stern abuse that he has been receiving since August 1986. He told an interviewer, "We do a show, [Howard] does an act . . . an act grows tired." He was also quoted as saying, "Howard Stern will find his first defeat at the hands of John DeBella." His overinflated ego really getting the best of him, he

added, "I'm *that* damn good." When Howard played this interview on the air, Gary Dell'Abate noted, "People with five
Oscars aren't this pompous." DeBella would soon learn that he
never should have drawn first blood with a competitor like
Stern.

As lame as the Morning Zoo was in Philadelphia, the ratings gave DeBella the power to insist that big names like Billy
Joel and others appear live on his show. It took a very confident
man to state on the air, as Howard did, that he would defeat
John DeBella in the ratings.

This prediction has come true. In April of 1990, Stern officially passed DeBella in the Arbitron Ratings book, which led
DeBella, who previously had said he would never lose to Stern
in the ratings, to state, "When Howard Stern has been number
one for five years, then he can say he's as good as me." Well,
it's 1994, and Howard is more popular than ever in
Philadelphia. He has received the city's highest ratings ever
and at one point was number one overall, surpassing the
"invincible" all-news KYW-AM. Not bad for a show that the
media said could never work in Philly because it originated
from New York. As Howard stated, Philadelphians "just want
good radio"; they don't care where it originates.

After surpassing DeBella in the ratings, Howard and crew
took off for the City of Brotherly Love to hold the funeral for the
"Zoo Keeper," an event they had promised their Philadelphia
audience ever since the first day they went on the air there.

The funeral day started with Howard holding his traditional press conference. (If you didn't already know this, a funeral
is one of the few occasions where Howard entertains the
media.) The press that day had no Dan Rathers or Mike
Wallaces in the crowd, and Howard asked, "Are there any
newspapers here that are not handwritten?" In his opening
remarks, Howard told the gathering of reporters, "We're proud
to be number one. I think it's well deserved. I've listened to the
Zoo Keeper's show, I think it's boring and dull, and I basically
think that this guy sucks and he should eat me. Everyone

should eat me." He went on to thank Philadelphians, especially for being the ones who turned him in to the FCC.

Thousands of Howard fans showed up in the rain to watch the Zoo Keeper's funeral. Howard, his crew, and his guests were greeted with a roar as they appeared on stage. Howard immediately started a "He sucks" chant and told the delirious crowd, "This jackass has been lingering like a bad fart in a Mexican locker room." Howard, who'd brought along a black gospel choir to back him up, began singing a version of "Amazing Grace" which contained such lyrics as "You embarrass yourself and your whole family, go hang yourself from a tree."

The balding Zoo Keeper was impersonated onstage by Scott "the Engineer" Salem, who looked like an exact duplicate while lying in a coffin in his sailor's cap, bushy mustache, and Hawaiian shirt. A Zoo Keeper doll was hung by the neck until "death" set in. Howard came out dressed like a bishop and Robin was dressed in a complete nun's outfit. Jessica Hahn and local Philadelphia celebrities such as Joe Frazier, Danny Bonaduce, and Miss Philadelphia also participated. Bonaduce, of *The Partridge Family*, appeared despite being a DJ at another Philadelphia radio station. Danny gave a touching "eulogy for the deceased" and ended with "Long live the king, Howard Stern," which had to make his employer at the time, radio station Eagle 106, wince in pain.

Another "eulogy" was delivered by "Reverend Jessie," who gave a speech that Martin Luther King Jr. would have been proud of. "Zoo Keeper at last, Zoo Keeper at last, thank God Almighty, Howard kicked your ass." They closed out the funeral by singing a listener's song that had won the Zoo Keeper song parody contest, which Howard had been running for months, "Baldy, Baldy." A takeoff on the unofficial Zoo theme, "Louie Louie," it went, "Baldy Baldy, whoa-oh-oh, your hair doesn't grow."

The most amazing thing that happened that day was that Howard correctly predicted to the Rittenhouse Square audience that not only would the Zoo Keeper's wife now divorce him, but she would also end up appearing on Howard's radio show for a Dial-a-Date.

One Stern fanatic whom DeBella couldn't seem to shake was a man known to listeners as "Captain Janks." He really is a captain, and was stationed in Panama during the invasion. He told *Philadelphia Magazine*, "When all the other guys were playing rock music outside of Noriega's house, I was blasting my Stern tapes. I'm a huge fan of Howard's."

Besides Howard, Captain Tom Janks was the worst nightmare for the Zoo Keeper. He is one of the many Stern fans who like to call up any talk show that takes listeners' calls and either ask a question or make a statement about Howard before the host cuts him off. Captain Janks's main target was John DeBella.

Philadelphia Magazine reported that on a day when the ratings came in showing Howard was increasing his lead over the Zoo Keeper, Captain Janks called the Zoo and complained that he was offended by a bit the Zoo Keeper had done regarding "vomit." He told the Zoo Keeper that "my sister died" when she choked on her own vomit. DeBella was in the middle of apologizing when Captain Janks asked, "And by the way, how does it feel to be a 7.4 versus a 10.3?" (These were the latest rating results.)

DeBella was not amused. Believing that Howard put the Captain up to these things, DeBella yelled, "Stern is a stain on the dial." Boy Gary replied to the charges that Howard was behind things: "There is a captain in Philadelphia who calls in regularly, but he is not associated with us and we don't tell him what to do. He just likes to call DeBella and annoy the crap out of him."

As annoying as the Captain can be, the most painful and humiliating moment for the Zoo Keeper has to have been when Howard's prediction of impending divorce came true for the Zoo Keeper. In January of 1992, his wife left him and he moved out of their house on the Main Line in Philly. Howard used the Zoo Keeper's marital problems to utterly humiliate the man.

Howard the gladiator with Jessica Hahn in Philadelphia for the "Baldy Divorce Party," 1992. (Alex Lloyd Gross/Star File)

In June of 1992, Howard returned to Philadelphia to throw a "Baldy Divorce Party." This time the real press showed up, including representatives of the local affiliates for both CBS and NBC. Howard's opening statement to the press that day was "Even though I made this guy's hair fall out, even though his wife divorced him, and even though I took his listeners, and even though I took his ratings and I took his `Louie Louie' theme, I vow to not rest until the Zoo Keeper is passed out drunk in a puddle next to a curb and the other bums are playing tic-tac-toe on top of his bald head."

Finally, it was time for Howard, who was dressed as a gladiator, to take the stage and greet his adoring fans. Again Stern, crew, and guests like Jessica Hahn and Howard's band, Pig Vomit, were welcomed by a roaring crowd. Howard compared the gathering to Woodstock, before starting the chant, "He's bald, she is gone . . . "

After a brief statement by Robin, Howard introduced Jessica, who was dressed in an outfit about which Robin said, "It's like her breasts were caught in a net." The outfit brought cheers from the crowd, while Howard stared at it and wondered, "Is that legal?"

After the song and addresses from both Stuttering John and Jackie Martling, Gary told the audience, "Now, back ten years ago I'm sure John DeBella thought I was a nobody. Well, I'm still a nobody, but I'm a nobody who works for Howard Stern with a 10 rating. . . . Drop dead, you bald, womanless jerk." I think this is a good lesson for all people in positions of power: Don't treat your underlings like shit; they may one day be in a position to pour some salt into open wounds.

Billy West sang a hilarious rendition of "Honey" and Fred Norris followed with an equally funny bashing of the Zoo Keeper, sung to "She's Gone." "He has lost most of his hair and his wife no longer cares," Fred sang with feeling, as a fitting end to the "Baldy Divorce Party." The Zoo Keeper's wife had not only left John DeBella, but also given Howard Stern a chance to revel in the fact that he had buried the onetime king of Philadelphia radio.

But even worse than that, Annette DeBella agreed to appear on the Howard Stern Show and do Dial-a-Date. Her boyfriend, Jack Godwin, told *Philadelphia Magazine* that Annette had originally agreed to go on the Stern show because John DeBella had "canceled her credit card" and she "needed" the $5,000 that Stern offered her to appear. Before the appearance, Annette called the Zoo Keeper's answering machine and threatened John with the Stern show: "You cancel my credit card and you want to be civil? Well, honey, listen to the radio next week. . . . I love you, too, you fat fucking bastard. . . . I'm so fucking glad I married you out of pity, it makes me sick."

During the Dial-a-Date, Howard was vicious toward his onetime radio rival. "I'm rubbing her back and kissing her neck, you stupid, bald idiot." Just when you thought it could not get any worse for the Zoo Keeper, you found out that one of the contestants playing for a date with his wife was none other than Captain Janks. It had to be fate, as the Zoo Keeper's wife selected Captain Janks for the date. Best of all, it was filmed and put on Howard Stern's videotape "Butt Bongo Fiesta." During the filming of the date, it became obvious that she was not at all opposed to the razzing that Howard was giving her ex. While in the back of a limo with Captain Janks, she asked if they should go by John's house, and she also gave us a very sarcastic "Yazoo" (DeBella's trademark, nonsensical saying).

Jack Godwin, brother of Pat Godwin, onetime Zoo sidekick, started dating Annette shortly after she left the Zoo Keeper, another slap in the face for DeBella. Jack told *Philadelphia Magazine* that Annette told him Howard Stern was "an absolute sweetheart" to her.

She did seem to enjoy the date, but obviously must have been keeping some real hurt hidden within her. In a really tragic twist, the Zoo Keeper's wife was found dead not long afterward. She was discovered in her car, which had been parked in the garage with the engine left running. It was an apparent suicide, although that theory has been disputed by both Jack Godwin and Annette's parents. John DeBella and her parents are both suing the bar which served Annette drinks on the night she died.

Philadelphia radio has not been the same since Howard Stern entered the market. The once-powerful Morning Zoo is gone. John DeBella was teamed up with Howard Eskin, who is a sports talk host, and just as annoying as DeBella, but the ratings dropped to a 2.9 and fourteenth place in the Philadelphia market. In April of 1993, WMMR canceled the DeBella/Eskin "sports-rock" experiment and DeBella quietly moved to afternoons. It was reported that WMMR's general manager, Chuck Fee, gave DeBella a choice between afternoons or the door. Some say DeBella took the afternoon job because "his agent was unable to find a better offer elsewhere."

DEBELLA'S LAST WORDS

In a final
interview before
leaving the Philadelphia airwaves, John DeBella told a reporter
for the local NBC affiliate that Howard
Stern had nothing to do with his departure
from radio. He went on to call Howard "a
great manipulator" and a "very good liar." (I
was just waiting for him to say "pants on
fire.") DeBella finished with this: "Stern takes
it to a level where some of it is not humor, it's
just cruel. . . . I'm not going to do that." No,
John, stick with the Zoo format. I'm sure
Philadelphians are going to demand
that you get back on the air one
"Gonzo Friday" to say
"Yazoo" real
soon.

Well, at least DeBella was no longer up against the man who had totally and completely destroyed him. There was no way Howard could humiliate the Zoo Keeper any further, was there? Well, as a matter of fact, there was. During the Zoo Keeper's first afternoon appearance, WYSP and Howard Stern ran a complete retrospective chronicling the downfall of the Zoo. This incensed WMMR's Fee, who complained to the *Philadelphia Inquirer*, "It's malicious." He went on to add, "Philadelphians are bored with Stern. . . . We're bored with you, Howard. . . . Stop boring us."

While Mr. Fee was spouting off, revealing that DeBella was not the only idiot at WMMR, the ratings were revealing that Philadephians love Stern and can't get enough of him. It's obvious that Howard had turned the entire WMMR staff into a bunch of whimpering losers.

In September of 1993, it was finally announced that the Zoo Keeper was leaving WMMR. The *Philadelphia Inquirer* reported that insiders were saying WMMR wanted to cut the onetime million-dollar DJ's salary down to $150,000. When he did not immediately accept, the station "yanked the offer off the table." Oh, well, "Good-bye, funny man"—to quote a favorite Howard phrase.

I think "the Philadelphia story" is a good indication of how lame radio across the country has been. Now that there is a real comedic talent available to people who don't want to just listen to news or music all day, we no longer have to put up with the juvenile schlock that was being dished up by the Morning Zoos and which had popped up on radio stations all across America. As Howard likes to say, "All Zoo Keepers are douche bags." Well, with the Philly Zoo Keeper taken care of, it was time for Howard to search out and destroy all the other weak morning DJs across the U.S.A.

CHAPTER 5

COAST TO COAST WITH HOWARD STERN

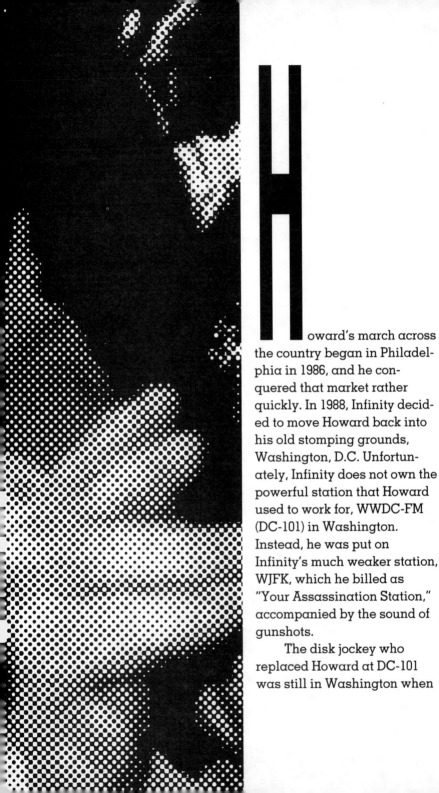

Howard's march across the country began in Philadelphia in 1986, and he conquered that market rather quickly. In 1988, Infinity decided to move Howard back into his old stomping grounds, Washington, D.C. Unfortunately, Infinity does not own the powerful station that Howard used to work for, WWDC-FM (DC-101) in Washington. Instead, he was put on Infinity's much weaker station, WJFK, which he billed as "Your Assassination Station," accompanied by the sound of gunshots.

The disk jockey who replaced Howard at DC-101 was still in Washington when

Howard arrived back on the air there. Doug "the Greaseman" Tracht had been unable to hold on to the high ratings that Howard originally brought to DC-101. However, being on the stronger radio network had allowed him to hold on to his lead over Howard in the ratings race in Washington.

This is one strange city. Washingtonians are the listeners who made Howard the star he is today, yet when he made his triumphant return "home" they did not embrace him in any manner worthy of his stature. Instead, they listened to a man who called himself "Greaseman."

The Greaseman is the same guy who created a character called "Sergeant Fury," who, according to him, was supposed to be "the story of my days in Vietman." The only problem with this concept is *the guy has never been there!!!*

This thirty-something DJ still somehow has managed to be embraced by the people in Washington, D.C., despite the fact that it's home to the Vietnam Veterans Memorial. In January 1993, Infinity, in a move that can only be described as "if you can't beat 'em, hire 'em," went out and hired the Greaseman as the 6-to-10-P.M. guy for its New York, Philadelphia, Washington, and Baltimore stations.

This strategy benefited both Infinity and Howard Stern almost immediately, as Howard soon took over the top morning spot in D.C. Unfortunately for the rest of us, it was at the cost of having to put up with the incessant ramblings of the Geekman . . . er, I mean Greaseman.

As a point of interest, to make room for the Greaseman, Meg Griffin, Howard's old sparring partner at K-Rock, reluctantly agreed to accept the overnight 10-to-2 time slot, which traditionally is the last slot offered before a DJ is kicked out the door.

Although Howard really wanted to make his return to Washington, D.C., there *was* one other market that appealed to him more than anyplace else—Los Angeles. It was the home of the DJs with the highest salaries yet the weakest shows—guys like Jay Thomas (the DJ Howard replaced on K-Rock), Rick Dees, and ratings kings Mark and Brian, the number one morning

In 1987, Jay Thomas—whom, you know as either Carla's hockey-playing husband, Eddie Lebeck, on *Cheers* (he ended up getting run over and killed), as Murphy Brown's ex-boyfriend and obnoxious TV counterpart on *Murphy Brown*, or from his more recent show, *Love & War* (originally costarring Susan Dey, who was then replaced by Annie Potts)—told the *Los Angeles Times*, "If [Howard] keeps getting dirtier, he's gonna lose his sponsors, his audience. If he goes clean, people are gonna say he's lost it." Not content with showing that he is a bad judge of talent, Thomas went on to show complete ignorance by talking about how New York City's audience may be hipper and more sophisticated, "but the kind of innuendo they enjoy over their morning coffee won't play west of the Hudson River." Let's hope the network that Jay works for doesn't let him start making program decisions, as he sounds about as bright as the old management team at WNBC. While we're at it, let's call a spade a spade: He was the worst actor on both *Cheers* and *Murphy Brown*. Who does this guy know in Hollywood?

team in L.A. at the time.

Howard *was* number one in New York and Philly, but critics and listeners alike still believed that his appeal would be limited to the Northeast. Regular guest and friend David Brenner said, "If he left New York, D.C., or Philadelphia, I think he'd be misunderstood. He'd be lynched."

Getting Howard into the Los Angeles market, which is still the most lucrative in the nation, was not as easy as it would appear, considering the scope of the Infinity empire. The Infinity-owned station in L.A. did not have a format that lent itself to Howard's brand of radio, so Infinity decided to license the Stern show to a

Howard arrives in Los Angeles. (Vincent Zuffante/Star File)

competitor. This strategy is unheard of in the radio industry. Howard is the first local radio personality who had proven "popular enough to have a show broadcast in more than one market at the same time on stations under different owner-ship." Greater Media Inc. was the competitor that decided to take the risk with Howard in L.A., reportedly paying Mr. Stern "millions of dollars" for this right. (It is unclear what the licens-ing fee was that Greater Media had to pay Infinity.) The deal also opened the door for the show to be licensed to other radio stations in cities where Infinity does not have a radio station.

Greater Media was gambling not only that Howard's brand of humor would be well received by the West Coast audi-ence, but also that listeners would accept the fact that Howard does bits specific to New York and the East Coast, as opposed

Howard makes his debut on KLSX in Los Angeles. (C.B.D. III/Star File)

to local L.A. news. For example: Would the L.A. audience be able to relate to a bit such as "The David Dinkins Speech School," where you can "learn to sound as white as Bryant Gumbel, O. J. Simpson, and Lester"?

Well, Greater Media took a great gamble when it decided to put Howard Stern on KLSX in Los Angeles. This station had been getting a 1.8 rating in the 6-to-10-A.M. time slot, which put it in a twenty-first place tie. Howard had a ways to go to beat Mark and Brian, who were then number one with a 7.5 rating.

Howard went on the air in Los Angeles in the fall of 1991. He told his new listeners, "First, I want to strip and rape Mark and Brian. I want my two bitches laying there in the cold, naked." If you'll remember, they had a really short-lived TV series on Sunday nights in which they did idiotic and very unfunny "Morning Zoo" stunts for TV. (It went on and off the air so quickly, it's doubtful anyone ever saw it.)

In one year's time, Howard Stern took his morning show from number twenty-one to number one in Los Angeles. During the fall of 1992, Howard vaulted past his "two bitches" with a 6.4 share, as compared to Mark and Brian's 5.6. If history actually

Howard performing "last rites" at the L.A. funeral for Mark and Brian, 1992. (Fred Blake/Star File)

does repeat itself—and in this case I'm sure it will—these two will soon be nowhere to be found on L.A. radio. Howard seems to be attending a lot of funerals these days. Not to worry—he always makes sure he gives his competition a decent burial.

One thing is certain: Eventually Mark and Brian will have nowhere to run and hide from Howard. Since his L.A. success, Infinity is having him take up market after market, including Cleveland, Dallas, Las Vegas, New Orleans, Buffalo, San Francisco, Miami, Rochester, and Albany. (He'd already gone on in Baltimore before beginning his show in L.A.)

Well, Howard the "street preacher" is now being heard by millions of fans across the country. For the benefit of Howard's new listeners, here are some examples of what you have been missing. But don't despair; "Best of Stern," the 6-to-10-A.M. broadcast of Stern show highlights that you'll hear whenever Howard decides to take a day or week off, is a good time to catch up on some of his best moments.

You could hear the sitcom spoof "Mayberry KKK," which has most of the townsfolk portrayed as Ku Klux Klan members. Who could ever forget Aunt Bee asking Barney, "How many boogies did you bag last night?" In this episode, Andy is the only nonracist in town and is shocked to hear Barney tell him, "I already bagged two Negras and a Jew." Unfortunately, even Andy succumbs to bigotry when he catches his lady friend, "Helen Crum," in bed with a black man.

Or this classic news analysis by Howard: "How can Jeffrey Dahmer get a fair trial unless there are more guys who want to have sex with dead men on the jury?"

Political commentary: "Boy, aren't those East Germans sorry-looking people? Don't they have any fresh fruit over there?"

Political commentary via the Stern show comes in all forms. Song parodies are probably the most entertaining way of getting across a political statement. In a song parody sung to the tune of "Addicted to Love," Howard got some jabs in at Supreme Court Justice Clarence Thomas. This song stated, "I gots a white wife who digs my big fudge, I might as well face it: I'm a Supreme Court stud."

Or you could be blessed with being able to hear "Larry Fine of the Three Stooges at Woodstock." In that routine, Larry yelled at the hippie crowd, "I had long hair before any of you jerkoffs. Get off those towers, you hard-ons . . . and somebody find me a whore."

If you ever do get to hear Larry of the Three Stooges on the *Howard Stern Show*, you'll notice that the voice sounds exactly like that of "Stimpy" of the *Ren and Stimpy* cartoon show that became an overnight sensation and then quickly turned into a cult classic. The reason for the similarity? It happens to be the same person doing both characters. That person is Billy West, another member of the Howard Stern team. A behind-the-scenes guy who does voices, he sometimes made appearances on Howard's TV show, most notably as Father Ritter of Covenant House fame.

Billy West's time is limited due to the work he does on *Ren and Stimpy* and other projects, so it is a treat when you do get to hear him perform on the Stern show. Howard, give us some

NOT HIS KIND OF TOWN: CHICAGO

As everyone
knows, in 1993 Chicago
lost one of its major public personalities due to unfortunate circum-
stances. No, I'm not talking about Michael
Jordan. Howard Stern began airing on
Chicago radio station WLUP-AM in 1992. By
August of 1993, the station had pulled the plug
on the budding superstar. The reason for the move
was not ratings. No, WLUP-AM stated that Stern's type
of humor "wasn't compatible with our station." It's incredible that a radio station can go out and hire someone
with the popularity and exposure of a Howard Stern and
not know what kind of humor it's going to be getting.
Howard has filed a lawsuit against WLUP-AM, and
Howard's agent, Don Buchwald, has told the press,
"Before we're through, it could turn out that Howard owns
an AM station in Chicago."
It is still way too early to tell how he is doing in all of the
new markets. But what we do know is that we are seeing
something totally unique to radio. *Time* magazine stated,
"Though talk show hosts like Rush Limbaugh and
Larry King have become hits across the country,
Stern is the first to dominate morning drive time
from coast to coast with what is essentially
a transplanted local program. His show
is full of New York news and personalities, yet listeners around the
country seem transfixed,
as if by some maniacal
visiting street
preacher."

more Larry Fine when you get a chance. It is Billy's best character, even better than that sound-alike Stimpy.

Okay, new fans, I won't lie to you. You do have to be prepared for the really disgusting stuff too. Like the belching contest that took place on the show between two female contestants, Janet and Tara. Not only was the premise of the contest foul, but the nasty bantering between the two contestants was even worse. "Are you giving points for blown chunks?" asked one of the contestants. "You smell like a yeast infection" was one of the retorts. Then finally, after Tara beat Janet with an extremely loud belch, Janet uttered this gem: "A bellyful of blown loads will get you every time." Come on, Janet, is that good sportsmanship?

Moving right along, you will find that Howard is at his absolute best when picking on other celebrities. Here's a bit I heard on "Best of Stern." After the *National Enquirer* ran a story alleging that Regis Philbin did not support a son of his who was confined to a wheelchair, Howard spoofed him on a bit called "Lifestyles of the Rich and Dicky." My favorite part was when Regis listened to his answering machine and heard Kathie Lee Gifford say, "Hi, this is Kathie Lee. My private parts itch, Regis. Should we do a segment on it?"

"Best of Stern" often highlights his specialty shows, such as the birthday bash Robin throws him every year. This is where celebrities come out and pay tribute to the "Radio God." Howard's band, Pig Vomit, usually plays at these events. This is also the band that does a lot of the song parodies, along with Fred Norris. Howard Stern's 1990 birthday bash featured such guests as Dennis Hopper, Phoebe Snow, rapper Young MC, and former New York City mayor Ed Koch, as well as an all-star band made up of Joe Walsh, Leslie West, and Southside Johnny.

He also received a phone call from his good buddy Sam Kinison, who was busy partying with Julian Lennon. In one of those "You never know what's going to happen next" moments, Howard put Julian on the phone with John Lennon's ex-mistress May Pang, who happened to be attending the celebration. This

CALLING DR. DEATH

Billy also played Dr. Jack Kevorkian on the TV show in a skit which told viewers to dial a specific 800 number if they were feelings depressed or were down-and-out. This bit caused a lady in New Jersey to file suit against Stern as intelligent fans began calling the phone number en masse; apparently, the number was for that of a vacation-home rental agency. If the lady had been clever, instead of suing Howard, she would have branched off into selling cemetery plots.

is exactly why listeners don't tune out!!

The Christmas shows are just as unique. Unfortunately, there is one you may never hear again, because the FCC has ruled that the entire broadcast was obscene. This was the show where Howard had on a black lesbian who stated she liked both black and white lesbians, because "it's all pink inside." On the same broadcast, "The Gay Choir" appeared and performed its version of "Winter Wonderland." The song contained several memorable lines, including, "Take my manhood, then lick my butt good" and "With a vise and some winches, We'll

Leslie West joins Howard at Mark and Brian's L.A. funeral. (Fred Blake/Star File)

stretch you to fourteen inches."

Later on in this Christmas show, Howard had a guest appear with a very special talent: He could play the piano with his penis. For him to do this, he needed an erection, so during the break he had to go into the bathroom and fondle himself. Unfortunately for him, while he was in there the general manager of WXRK walked in and caught the guy playing with himself, which almost put an end to the broadcast. Howard somehow managed to get the situation under control, and still brought the guy out and had him play the piano with his penis. The music was okay, but not great.

If you ever want to hear this show, you should track down someone who purchased Howard's CD/cassette "Crucified by the FCC," because it probably will never be aired again.

CHAPTER 6

CRUCIFIED BY THE F.C.C. AND THE RELIGIOUS RIGHT

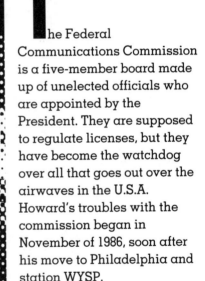

he Federal
Communications Commission
is a five-member board made
up of unelected officials who
are appointed by the
President. They are supposed
to regulate licenses, but they
have become the watchdog
over all that goes out over the
airwaves in the U.S.A.
Howard's troubles with the
commission began in
November of 1986, soon after
his move to Philadelphia and
station WYSP.

It seems that the
Philadelphia airwaves were
being monitored by someone
connected to a group called
the "National Federation for
Decency," based in Tupelo,
Mississippi. This organization

is headed by the Reverend Donald Wildmon, a fifty-five-year-old United Methodist minister. Mr. Wildmon describes his group as "a Christian organization promoting the biblical ethic of decency in the media," a claim that should have prompted the FCC to leave Howard alone; ever hear of separation of church and state? The FCC, however, decided to play God.

In a lengthy letter to Infinity sent in the fall of 1986, the FCC charged WYSP with obscenity and indecency on its morning radio show. This was the first time in eight years that the FCC had used the obscenity issue to target a radio station. Up until the 1986 letter, the issue had been clear: The FCC had taken the position, and the U.S. Supreme Court had agreed, that broadcasters were prohibited from using seven "dirty" words.

With the charges lodged against Infinity and two California stations for their own "offenses," it became clear that the FCC was drastically changing its definition of what was "obscene." In April of 1987, the FCC announced that it was going to "correct an altogether-too-narrow interpretation of decency." The commission put the nation's 12,000 radio and television stations on notice of the change. Under its new approach, the FCC targeted "language or material that depicts or describes, in terms patently offensive as measured by contemporary community standards for the broadcast medium, sexual or excretory activities or organs."

This was a vague declaration with no specific regulations. Let's face it, we have a group of unelected officials pretty much going way beyond a ruling by the Supreme Court of the United States on their own. They are getting away with it despite the fact that their action has First Amendment crusaders up in arms. The FCC ruling is an attack on us, Howard's fans. It is also an attack against our First Amendment right of free speech.

Members of the broadcasting industry did nothing to support their colleague under fire from the FCC. Rick Dees was profiled in the *Los Angeles Time* as "being amused" by the FCC ruling, stating that the FCC has a "hit list" of people like

THE SEVEN DIRTY WORDS

These words were made quite famous by comedian George Carlin in a routine called "The Seven Words You Can Never Say on Television." They are "shit," "piss," "cunt," "fuck," "cocksucker," "motherfucker," and "tits." Carlin's routine is hilarious, as he states that there are 400,000 words in the English language and you are allowed to say 399,993 of them. Mr. Carlin also can't understand how "tits" got lumped in with the rest of the "dirty" words. "It's such a happy word," he observes, "almost like a snack."

Howard and Robin are joined by Lisa Sliwa and other Guardian Angels at the FCC rally, New York City, 1987. (Chuck Pulin/Star File)

Howard Stern. Boy, there is a crusader for free speech! No wonder his show blows.

Howard has millions of fans out there who do not find him the least bit objectionable, or when a teensy bit objectionable, not enough so to make us turn the dial. On the other hand, the FCC lodged a complaint against Howard Stern based on the fact that it had received a grand total of thirty-five complaints against Howard—most of them made by the same group. At the time, Howard had over half a million listeners in Philadelphia alone!! Is this the minority ruling the majority or what!?!

What was the focus of these few complaints? In a booklet that Howard included with "Crucified by the FCC," there are six excerpts taken directly from the memorandum that the FCC sent to Infinity. Five of the six excerpts deal specifically with conversations held by "Bob and Ray," as played by Howard Stern and Robin Quivers. Here they are in order of appearance.

Excerpt 1

Bob (Howard): "God, my testicles are like down to the floor. Boy, baby, you could really have a party with these. I'm telling you, honey."

Ray (Robin): "Use them like boccie balls.

Excerpt 2

Bob: "Let me tell you something, honey. Those homos you are with are all limp."

Ray: "Yeah. You've never even had a real man."

Howard Stern: "You've probably never been with a man with a full erection."

Excerpt 3

Woman: "No, I was in a park in New Rochelle, New York."

Bob: "In a park in New Rochelle? On your knees?"

Woman: "No, no."

Ray: "And squeezing someone's testicles, probably."

Excerpt 4
(Talking to a caller)

Howard Stern: "I'd ask your penis size and stuff like that, but I really don't care."

Excerpt 5
(As part of a discussion of lesbians)

Bob: "I mean to go around porking other girls with vibrating rubber products and *they* [lesbians] want the whole world to come to a standstill."

Excerpt 6

Bob: "Have you ever had sex with an animal?"

Caller: "No."

Howard and "Grampa" Al Lewis at the FCC rally. (Chuck Pulin/Star File)

Bob: "Well, don't knock it. I was sodomized by Lamb Chop—you know, that puppet Shari Lewis holds?"

Bob: "Baaaaaah. That's where I was thinking that Shari Lewis would never have to sodomize anyone. She could have Lamb Chop do it."

Howard's response to the FCC's attack on him was to hold a protest rally outside the United Nations building in New York City. On April 24, 1987, five thousand people showed up in support of free speech and heard a memorable exchange between Howard Stern and "Grampa" Al Lewis of *The Munsters* fame. This particular broadcast was going out live over the airwaves—without the usual seven-second delay—because it was being done on location. "Grampa" began to talk with the audience, asking them why they had gathered there, when Howard interjected, "Why is that, Grampa? So you can get young boys?" "Grampa" denied that suggestion and then proclaimed to the entire listening audience, "We're here because we all have a purpose in being here, and that purpose is to say, *Fuck the FCC!!*" The crowd began chanting "Fuck the FCC," as Howard and Robin panicked, knowing that the broadcast was *live*.

In all his battles with the FCC, Howard has had the complete backing of Infinity and its president, Mel Karmazin. In response to the initial charges against Howard, Karmazin said, "Howard Stern is a comedian. He does humor." He also stated, "These letters are part of what appears a crusade on the part of Mr. Wildmon."

Allen Wildmon, the brother of Donald and public relations director of the National Federation for Decency, responded in the *Los Angeles Times*, "People give you the simplistic answer that all you've got to do is reach up and turn it off. Reaching up and turning it off is like walking down the street and seeing a rape, turning your head, and walking on by. You don't get involved." Wildmon needs a talking to; he has compared the voluntary act of listening to a humorous radio show to forcible rape.

Eventually, Howard Stern was cleared of any wrongdoing connected with the FCC charges of 1986. No fines were levied against Howard or Infinity Broadcasting. However, the FCC had successfully put into place those new and vague guidelines, which would force more showdowns later on.

Not long after, the FCC came back for another shot at Howard. This time, Howard did not get off as easily. In November of 1990, the FCC imposed fines of $6,000 against Infinity. The fines were $2,000 each for three radio stations that carried Howard's show. These fines were imposed because of the 1988 broadcast of the Christmas show that featured the man playing a piano with his penis. What caused the FCC to really blow a gasket was when Howard described the "big black lesbian out of her mind with lust."

Does the FCC watch daytime television? Oprah, Phil, Geraldo, Sally, and the rest of the daytime talk shows discuss such subjects as orgasm, penis size, adultery, rape, incest, men who dress like women, etc., etc., etc. Because Howard has a comedy show, he is not allowed to talk about these subjects. That is completely ridiculous, and the FCC commissioners

Howard and Leslie West at the FCC rally. (Chuck Pulin/Star File)

should be ashamed of themselves for taking their own personal tastes and forcing them down the throats of every American.

The FCC should realize that normal Americans are smart enough to change the channel when we're offended. However, it's obvious that the people who are members of the National Federation for Decency are not that smart; they listen to Howard constantly and write down every word he says!

The FCC was still not finished with Howard. In October of 1992, it announced the largest-ever penalty for an "indecent broadcast." Then, in January of 1993, the commission topped its previous record penalty, imposing an unheard-of fine of $600,000 on WXRK in New York, WYSP in Philly, and WJFK in Washington, D.C. In August 1993, the FCC added another $500,000 fine, bringing the Stern penalties to well over a million dollars. Infinity continues to refuse to pay any of it. The FCC attack on America's favorite radio personality has now become a personal attack on the millions of fans who listen to and love Howard every day of the week. The FCC wants to stop you from having a laugh in the morning as you sit in traffic waiting to put your time in at work.

The following is a sample of statements by Howard from eight broadcasts cited by the FCC when it imposed its outrageous fines.

1● Oct. 30, 1991—Concerning Pee Wee Herman's trial for public indecency at an adult theater in Florida, Stern said, "Let me tell you this: If they are going to make him do public service, the service should be, he should go to every movie theater in Sarasota and scrub the theater seats where guys drop their load. Because I'm going to tell you something—that's disgusting. Imagine: I go to the movie theater and I'm sitting in Pee Wee's mess."

2● Oct. 31, 1991—"The closest I came to making love to a black woman was when I masturbated to a picture of Aunt Jemima." Guest Geraldo Rivera replied, "Oh, come on." Howard continued, "On a pancake box. All right? . . . I did it right on her kerchief."

3● Nov. 5, 1991—Concerning Pee Wee Herman having masturbated twice within ten minutes: "I, who am the head of the masturbator club, I run a masturbation society. I am someone totally devoted to masturbation. I must tell you, to do that twice in ten minutes is unbelievable."

4● Nov. 4, 1991—"First, I want to strip and rape Mark and Brian. I want my two bitches laying there in the cold, naked . . . I want them bleeding from the buttocks."

5● Nov. 15, 1991—"Hey, FCC: penis . . . I do draw the line at vagina. Whoa, I can't believe I just said that word." On Michelle Pfeiffer: "I would not even need a vibrator . . . Boy, her rump would be more black and blue than a Harlem cub scout."

6● Nov. 17, 1991—Again on Mark and Brian: "Two little pussies with dildos."

7● Nov. 20, 1991—To Robin: "Let me tell you something, since we found out that you like sex where the rest of us wipe . . . "

8● Nov. 27, 1991—To *Knots Landing* actress Stacy Galina: "Hey, I've done stuff to myself and thought about you."

It seems to me that the FCC has a problem with masturbation. However, you can hear Dr. Ruth talk about masturbation on numerous shows during various times of the day. Howard is being targeted, and it is starting to affect him. After the Los Angeles fine was announced, he was quoted in *Broadcasting and Cable* magazine as saying, "It's a black day for the Stern show." Later he said the FCC is "targeting me because I'm the most visible guy" and that it is "trying to put a dead stop on my career. The U.S. government says `go after Stern,' there's nothing you can do about it. You can't fight the government."

The most disturbing attack on Howard was the one launched by Howard Tanger, president and CEO of Marlin Broadcasting. In November of 1992, he initiated an anti-Howard Stern campaign "to rally the radio industry and force Stern off the air." The drive began on WFLN in Philadelphia, which called Stern "reprehensible and irresponsible . . . abusive and obnoxious" in a radio editorial. Tanger had also written to the National Association of Broadcasters and to members of the Clinton administration, asking them for support in ridding the airwaves of Howard. "He is just going to ruin it for the radio industry," Tanger wrote, according to *Broadcasting* magazine.

This sounds to me like a ploy to attack Infinity, which is quickly becoming the most powerful broadcasting empire in the history of radio.

Tanger's motives for this despicable attack on Howard

Stern may never be known, but it is clear that people like Howard Tanger are the biggest enemies of the First Amendment. This is a guy who owns a company in an industry whose entire foundation is built on free speech, but he is attacking someone who is utilizing his inalienable right to this freedom. Does Mr. Tanger realize that in 1776, the British thought the colonists were "reprehensible," "irresponsible," "abusive," and "obnoxious"? Our forefathers went on to fight the British so that we could have certain freedoms, one of which was freedom of speech.

If Mr. Tanger was hoping that the FCC would block the sale of three more radio stations to Infinity Broadcasting, it didn't work. In a vote of 4 to 1, the FCC decided in January of 1993 that Infinity could buy stations in Boston, Chicago, and Atlanta. The one dissenting vote, of course, was cast by former FCC chairman Alfred Sikes. He may still have been holding a grudge over the fact that after it was announced that he was battling cancer, Howard stated on his radio show that he hoped Sikes's cancer spread. Infinity apologized for this remark. On the other hand, I don't think Infinity ever apologized for Howard's statement that he hoped Howard Tanger died in an auto accident. Although the FCC ended up approving the sale of the three stations to Infinity, this happened only after the company stipulated that the *Howard Stern Show* would not air on any of its new stations. How blatant can the FCC get about targeting Howard?

HOWARD STERN: THE COMEDIC GENIUS

SAM AND JESSICA

Howard often has celebrities either come into the studio or call in to plug their latest movie, album, or upcoming public appearance. That was never the case with Sam Kinison and Jessica Hahn. These two deserve their own chapter simply because they are the best two guests *ever* to appear on the *Howard Stern Show*. The two things that both of them had in common were their infamous backgrounds with religion and Howard Stern.

Let's start with the late Sam Kinison. He easily qualified as the most interesting, controversial, and hilarious guest ever to appear on

Sam Kinison: the greatest Stern guest ever.

Howard's show. Every time Sam entered the WXRK studio, things seemed to get wild.

Sam Kinison was born on December 7, 1953. His big break came at the hands of Rodney Dangerfield, who booked Sam for his 1985 HBO special. The next year Sam was in Dangerfield's hit movie, *Back to School*, playing the "schizoid" history professor. Sam's career shot out of control after that. He cut his first album, "Louder Than Hell," hosted *Saturday Night Live* and the MTV Awards, appeared on all of the late-night talk shows, including Letterman four times, and sold out major venues during his "Thunder and Lightning" tour of 1987.

Yes, 1987 was the year in which Sam Kinison's career took off like a bolt of lightning and he became a "superstar." That same year, a North Carolina paper broke the story of a scandalous motel rendezvous between a famous TV evangelist and a church secretary. The secretary's name was Jessica Hahn.

She was born in 1959, and grew up in Massapequa, New York, a middle-class town on Long Island. When Jessica turned twenty years old, a preacher by the name of John Fletcher invited her to a Praise the Lord (PTL) telethon in Florida. It was at a motel during her stay in Florida that John Fletcher introduced Jessica to Jim Bakker (husband of Tammy Faye), whom she had idolized for years. It was also there that the two preachers allegedly drugged and raped Jessica, who, according to her, was a virgin at the time.

Once the news report of the tryst and cover-up hit, life for Jessica, Jim, and Tammy Faye was never the same. Jessica locked herself up in her West Babylon, Long Island, trailer apartment, attempting to avoid the horde of reporters that camped outside her home.

Howard, who is known for trying to reach people in the news via the telephone, called Jessica and, for those savvy enough to read between the lines, offered support and much-needed friendship.

"With all his craziness, he was the only one to call and say, `Jessica, are you okay?' He's a decent man," Jessica insisted. And even though there are people out there who will accuse Howard of using Jessica for his own gain, Howard has never turned his back on her. Long after the Donna Rices and Fawn Halls of the world disappeared from the public eye, Howard kept Jessica's name alive by having her on his radio and TV shows, as well as making her part of his video projects.

She, for her part, has stood by Howard, even in the face of ridicule. During her appearance on *Donahue*, right after the scandal broke, Jessica stated that it was Howard Stern who had helped her through the rough times. Despite the outraged reaction of Phil Donahue and his audience, she stuck by her guns and made it clear that Howard *had* come through for her, and had no intention of exploiting her.

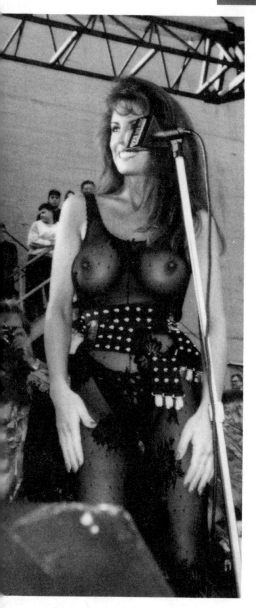

Jessica in Los Angeles, 1992. (Fred Blake/Star File)

Jessica's life began to turn around when she latched on to a Long Island divorce attorney, Dominic Barbara. (Fans of Howard will know that Dominic has gone on to become good friends with Howard, attending Super Bowl parties and card games with him.) Barbara played a vital role as advisor to Jessica during the very difficult period when the media was all over her for interviews. Probably his one mistake was not talking Jessica out of the *Donahue* appearance. What Barbara did do was steer Jessica in the direction of *Playboy*'s main playboy, Hugh Hefner.

Hefner paid Jessica a substantial sum of money for the interview and photo shoot that caused such a stir in 1987. And the November '87 issue was one of the magazine's bestselling ever. Jessica revealed that Jim Bakker told her, "When you help the shepherd, you're helping the sheep." (Now there's a pickup line for all you up-and-coming TV evangelists out there.) She also revealed that he uttered this

HOWARD AND THE "BON PHONEY" FEUD

Bon Jovi used to appear on Howard's show when it was a group that no one had ever heard of. Howard would bring the band members in and play their music and predict big things for them one day. When they finally did break out and become a smash in the music world, they stopped appearing on the show for some time. Jon Bon Jovi blames this on his record label for having put pressure on him to stay off the Stern show. However, it seems to me that a group of Bon Jovi's stature should have had enough balls to make a stand against monetary blackmail. Rock stars are supposed to be rebels, not sniffling little wimps. (Howard finally did forgive the group for stiffing him for all those years when they appeared on one of his birthday extravaganzas.)

During one appearance, which I remember as being superb, Sam came in and told Howard that he had a surprise set up for the next day. He was going to bring Bon Jovi in for a reunion with Howard. Howard had no reason to doubt Sam, as they had become good friends. The next day, beginning at 6 A.M., Howard, Robin, and millions of fans (including myself) got up to await the arrival of Bon Jovi and the big reunion, clash, or whatever it was going to be. It was the kind of radio that has made Howard as popular as he is; it even got attention from the press.

Well, we waited and waited and waited, and Howard was getting angrier and angrier. At around 9 A.M. it became clear to Howard that he had been set up, and he began leveling off on both Sam and Bon Jovi. He called Sam a "Big Fat Cow" and just about every other derogatory name in the book. Sam could not have realized what a big mistake he had made. Howard's fans were livid; we all felt betrayed by someone we had grown to know and love. Sam not only became the focus of daily attack by Howard, but was also hounded by Stern fans wherever he performed. It was during this time that Howard proclaimed Andrew "Dice" Clay to be the funniest comedian he knew. We all realized it was a lie, but we didn't care. Sam had hurt us.

MR. ED MEETS JESSICA HAHN

The skit was set in a private plane and opened with Jessica thanking the talking horse for putting her in his video, "Wild Horses." It's only seconds before passion overtakes Jessica and her large stud Ed (played by Howard) asks her for her "snappin' gyro." As Jessica and the Stallion get it on, it really starts to get hot and heavy. "Another hoof. Oh God, another hoof. Ed, another hoof, another hoof," Jessica cries out in the heat of passion. When Mr. Ed informs the delirious Hahn that he has run out of hooves, she asks the talking horse to "gallop." Jessica, incredibly excited, at this point begins moaning the theme song to the old Mr. Ed show, but soon becomes aware that her four-legged Romeo is awfully quiet. When she realizes Ed has fallen asleep, she yells, "You bastid! Get off me, Ed."

gem: "Tammy Faye is too big and cannot satisfy me." Gosh, I can almost see the mascara running down her face after she read that one.

Back to Sam, who, as most people know, was a real-life preacher who once spread the gospel himself. As his popularity had risen, he'd gained a reputation as the "rock 'n' roll comedian," making friends with the likes of Billy Idol, Eric Clapton, Motley Crue, and of course, Bon Jovi. He had also had some fabulous radio moments on the *Howard Stern Show* and had become great friends with Howard, whom he described as the "Radio God."

Sam called in the next day and the two comedic giants had it out on the air. Sam told Howard that the Bon Jovi scam was a "show business kind of gag" and that he "didn't know you were going to freak out and turn on me like a rabid dog, man." Sam and Howard went at it in a brutal manner for a good fifteen minutes before Sam hung up.

It was about this time that Sam and Jessica ended the brief fling they had over the summer of 1988. Even as Sam Kinison's career took off and Jessica did daily battle with the media, they met and had an affair. Unfortunately, the affair turned rather nasty. Jessica revealed to Howard that Sam had "fallen asleep insider her" after a night of heavy drinking. She also charmingly recalled that he once lost control of his bowels and took a dump on the carpet in a hotel room.

Sam denied ever having left his "calling card" on the carpet of some hotel but joked about it on the Stern show anyway. "That's a sexual signature of mine," he once told Howard. "Some guys like to leave flowers, other guys like to leave perfume, money; I like to just take a dump."

Howard had his falling-out with Sam just as Jessica and Sam ended their torrid romance, and Howard, never one to miss an opportunity, asked Jessica to participate in a bit of fun. Jessica and Sam's stormy affair was lampooned on Howard's show in a skit entitled, "Mr. Ed meets Jessica Hahn." In this radio sketch, Jessica played herself.

Fortunately for all Stern fans, the Stern-Kinison feud did not last long, as Sam could not resist calling Howard to pledge money for a radiothon that Howard was holding for Regis Philbin's "flipper-footed" son. Soon after that, Sam was back in the studio to clear the air over the entire Bon Jovi affair. Howard, of course, realized that this was what his fans had been waiting for, and we were not disappointed one bit. You could feel the tension in the studio as soon as Sam arrived.

Howard let "Ronnie the Limo Driver" express the sentiments of the millions of fans who felt that Sam had stabbed Howard in the back. Ronnie called in and told Sam that he is a "user," that he used Howard and he used Jessica. Sam responded by saying that he was not the one who put her in a sketch where she had sex with a horse. He went on to mention that someone should ask Jessica what her sales from the "Wild Thing" poster are. ("Wild Thing" was the hit song and video remake of the Troggs classic that Sam made with Jessica Hahn and a host of rock stars. Sam called it "a gang-rape fantasy of all the metal rock groups against organized religion.)

Sam then said that he realized he had offended "devout Howard fans. . . . I made a big mistake; it was my fault. I was out of line. I didn't know it would blow up and be this kind of crisis."

That probably could have been the end of it, but unfortunately for Jessica—and fortunately for the people listening that day—she decided to call in just as Sam was finishing up his apology. The original purpose of Jessica's phone call was to dispute Sam's claim that she had made a lot of money off the sale of "Wild Thing" posters. It also only took her about two seconds before she let Sam know that she thought Ronnie the Limo Driver was correct in implying that Sam had used her.

When Sam heard that Jessica felt "used" by him, the fun really began. "I used you, Jessica? Give me a break. I'm not Jim Bakker, babe. Pull that line on somebody else," Sam countered. He went on to accuse her of planting a story in the *National Enquirer*, of being too stupid to have turned her video appearance into a movie career, of putting out a "Wild Thing" poster without his "permission," and of being just plain "mean" to him. Yes, folks, this was live radio at its finest.

Moving right along, Sam then accused Howard of making fun of his brother Kevin's suicide. I'm not sure what Howard said or if he said anything at all about the suicide of Sam's mentally depressed brother, who walked into his mother's house and shot himself in the head. "[Howard] didn't know that I tried to save him for two years, and I put him in rehab, and that he'd blow his brains out and it's not a joke, man . . . joke about Pat Cooper's family, joke about Regis Philbin's son with the flipper feet, but not my little brother Kevin that I tried to save and I lost," Sam pleaded. The radio broadcast of the *Hindenburg* disaster was beginning to pale in comparison to the intensity of this conversation.

The most vicious line of the conversation came from Sam at the expense of Jessica. "Do another Mr. Ed routine, babe, while your mom's dying, all right?" Sam offered as he went for the jugular. At this point, Jessica broke down sobbing and tried to say that she had done the Mr. Ed bit *before* her mother passed away. Howard immediately got Jessica off the line as he realized that Sam was out of control and was not going to show any mercy. With Jessica off the line, Sam turned his attention to Howard and screamed at him, "*Come on, be funny, man. Come on, Howard!!!*" Robin, not missing a beat, said, "Well, are we making up or what!"

Amazingly enough, things quieted down in the studio rather quickly, and it was not long before Sam and Howard were discussing what "great radio" had just occurred. I'm not so sure Jessica would have agreed with them but as Sam put it, "This is the kind of stuff Imus has wet dreams about. . . . " It was a real-life soap opera.

Sam was fighting with everyone, and everyone was fighting with Sam. Shortly after Jessica and he battled via the Stern airwaves, Leslie West, the legendary guitarist of Mountain, and Sam went at it on Howard's radio show. Apparently, Leslie was

Sam with Dee Snyder, Leslie West, and one of his "babies" at the Felt Forum in New York City. (Chuck Pulin/Star File)

mad at Sam for not having allowed him to produce "Wild Thing," after Sam had promised it to him, and Sam was mad at Leslie for having been the only performer to demand money for a benefit concert for legendary comedian Lenny Bruce's mother. The amazing thing about the on-air dispute was that the extremely large Leslie West had the gall to call Sam a "fat son of a bitch" before hanging up on him.

Soon after all of these heated confrontations, Howard and Sam made up for good, as did Sam and Leslie. Eventually even Sam and Jessica would let bygones be bygones. But over a period of a few months, Stern fans had been treated to some of the most intense radio they could ever hope to hear. Sam was absolutely correct in stating that Howard knew this was great radio. Stern has a knack of being able to get people to talk on the air as if they were having a conversation in the privacy of their own home. That, among many other qualities, sets him head and shoulders above everyone else.

After the broadcast of the Sam-and-Jessica conversation, Jessica went back to doing a stint with an Arizona radio station. She actually was a part of the Y-95 Morning Zoo, where she read horoscopes and told Hollywood gossip. She also had her teeth capped, her nose slimmed, and her breasts enlarged, in part for a syndicated TV show called *Jessica Hahn's Love Line*. She also showed off her new body in the September 1988 issue of *Playboy*.

One other business venture Jessica was involved in was a 900 number on which she would leave a message each day to anyone who cared to hear her. Well, Howard did, and he would call up and make fun of the message, along with Jessica's "snappin' gyro." All of a sudden, the same person who had played herself in a bit in which she made love to a horse was offended by her good friend and Mr. Ed costar, Howard Stern. She called up and left a message on Gary's answering machine saying how upset she was, adding that Howard was now "dead to me." She went on to say, "I'm fucking mad at you people. . . . Next time you guys need a favor, call somebody else."

Howard's reaction to the message from Jessica was not one of empathy. As a matter of fact, he gave her "forty seconds" to call up and apologize to him! (Howard's point, I think, was that he had made Jessica into a star.) But Howard backed off his Jessica is "dead to us" stance and broke down and called her. The first phone call didn't go too well, as Howard insulted her again and she hung up, but he called her right back. During that second call, Howard told her, "I respect you, I love you, and I'll never fall asleep in you." Jessica eventually came to her senses.

Jessica continues to be a favorite guest of Howard's and is willing to help him in just about any way possible. Howard's video, "Butt Bongo Fiesta," features Jessica in a totally see-through body stocking. That alone is worth the price of the video.

Jessica, Leslie West, and Howard in L.A., 1992. (Fred Blake/Star File)

Sam's career reached its peak with the release of his second album, "Have You Seen Me Lately?" This was the album that contained the hit song "Wild Thing." It was also Sam Kinison at his most outrageous, and most offensive. The album contains tracks like "Rock Against Drugs" ("That's like Christians against Christ"). He offended MADD (Mothers Against Drunk Driving) with his bit on drinking and driving. "It's not like you're going to your car thinking, 'Well, I sure hope I slide into a family of six tonight.'" He went on to use his primal scream to deliver "But there's no other way to get our fucking car back to the house.'"

He offended the entire homosexual and medical community in one fell swoop with his bit about AIDS. "Safe sex, get off our back. Because a few fags fuck some monkeys . . . they got so bored, their own assholes weren't enough." He then joked about the AIDS public-service announcement: "Aren't you afraid of

AIDS? . . . Heterosexuals die of it, too." Sam's response, in his trademark Scream: "*Name One!!! . . .* It's not our dance."

There is also a track entitled "The Story of Jim." A "hypocritical, self-righteous bastard" is how Sam described the disgraced evangelist. Sam continued, "Jesus is up in heaven saying, 'Where the fuck did I say to build a water slide?'" referring to the home/amusement park that Jim Bakker built using PTL funds. He added, "If you're going to lose a kingdom over some pussy, this is the girl," referring to Jessica Hahn. He also takes some swipes at Jessica for agreeing to pose in *Playboy.*

At the end of the album, you are rewarded with Sam's much-talked-about remake of "Wild Thing." Sam's version of the song includes these classic lines: "Eery time I kiss you, I taste what another guy had for lunch"; "You're a wild, unfaithful, untrustable tramp, and I think I love you"; "I'll never forget you. You used me. Why didn't you tell me you were a demon from hell?"

There you have it: Sam's own personal tribute to women.

Sam's album led to attacks on him from every group imaginable. According to *Rolling Stone* magazine, Sam's response to the homosexuals who attacked his AIDS rap was, "They say I'm not sensitive. Sensitive? Aren't you the same guys that tape up gerbils and shove them up your ass?" To the medical community: "They say my jokes aren't medically correct. They don't have to be. They're not prescriptions, they're fucking jokes." The protests against Sam were very much like the kinds of things Howard must deal with on a daily basis. As Sam stated quite clearly, "They're fucking jokes."

By 1988, Sam's career was on a major downslide. His drug and alcohol intake was beginning to catch up with him. He also saw a movie deal with United Artists fall through. In between all this, Sam was still making some amazing appearances on the *Howard Stern Show.* On one visit, he and his future wife, Malika Souri, discussed their preference for "three-way sex; four is bad choreography, five a sports event." He also had a phone showdown with fellow comic Bobcat Goldthwait, of

Police Academy fame. Howard set up the conversation as a chance to bring peace between the two feuding comics. However, it turned into a Sam blitzkrieg of Bobcat, who ended up bailing out with a hang-up.

Outside of the Stern show, things couldn't have gotten much worse for Sam. In 1990, his last album, "Leader of the Banned," was not selling and an HBO special was canceled. One night Sam had to be rushed to the hospital after sniffing some bad cocaine. He was also diagnosed as having an irregular heartbeat. Then, in the early morning of June 21, 1990, Sam lay passed out in his house while a bodyguard whom he had apparently hired the night before was upstairs allegedly raping Malika. Sam was so out of it that he did not hear Malika's screams for help, nor the gunshots she fired at her alleged attacker. Howard would later tell Sam, "Some of your other bodyguards looked like they would rape me." Sam Kinison could not have sunk much lower. However, it was this episode that began the process of changing Sam's life.

Sam was beginning to clean up his life after the alleged rape. He had joined Alcoholics Anonymous and was off drugs. After landing a guest role on *Married With Children*, he ended up with a starring role on the Fox TV show *Charlie Hoover*. He had even signed a deal to make two movies.

However, Sam would never be able to give up his wild lifestyle for any period of time. He caused a big stir when he became "too drunk" to appear on *The Joan Rivers Show*. Joan had planned to devote the entire show to him. Instead, she ended up calling Howard Stern and asking him questions about Sam. (Sam had appeared on Howard's show earlier in the day.) The show was to be about Sam being a rebel comic, and Sam was apparently just proving that he was still a rebel. Joan was not amused, and ended up trying to track him down at his hotel. The tabloid shows had a field day with the incident, which Sam blamed on "bad Chinese food."

It took Howard the mediator to hook Sam and Joan up on his radio show, where Sam apologized to Joan and promised to make another appearance on her show.

Sam and Howard seemed to always be able to create magic on the radio together, and there was obviously a mutual love and respect between them. Sam once told Howard, "I'd do your sister if I didn't think it would affect our relationship." Howard replied, "I'd be honored to have you do my sister." (I wonder if Ellen would have been so "honored"?) Sam would always make it clear that Howard Stern's was the only radio show he would appear on. "I pledge my allegiance and my soul to the Stern show," he stated on one of his many appearances.

On April 5, 1992, Sam Kinison married longtime girlfriend Malika Souri in a ceremony in Las Vegas. Things, once again, had turned around for Sam. In Sam's own words, he was again "set up for the next tragedy." Unfortunately for Sam, this tragedy would be his last.

In what can only be described as a cruel twist of fate, Sam Kinison lost his life in an auto accident on April 10, 1992, only five days after his marriage to Malika. After a quick honeymoon in Hawaii, Sam had returned to do three sold-out shows in Laughlin, Nevada. At around 7:30 P.M., near Needles, California, on the drive to Laughlin, a pickup truck headed in the opposite direction suddenly crossed the dividing line and crashed head-on into the white Trans Am that Sam was driving on U.S. 95. Sam's brother Bill; his personal assistant, Majid Khoury; and his longtime friend and fellow comic, Carl LeBove, were following behind Sam and saw the accident firsthand. When they reached Sam, he was lying across an unconscious Malika, who had been riding in the passenger seat.

According to *Esquire* magazine, Sam was conscious and he muttered to Majid, "I don't understand it. I don't understand it. How come now? . . . How come?" Although he was told not to move, Sam struggled out of the car. Carl grabbed him before he fell. While he lay on the ground, his head cradled by Carl, he said, "Don't understand. Why now?" Sam seems to have received an answer to this question from someone whom only Sam could see. His last words were "Okay . . . okay . . . " only

Sam's last live in-studio appearance on the *Howard Stern Show* was also one of his best. During that broadcast, he described to Howard how he told Malika that he had been having an affair with her sister, Sabrina, for a year and a half. He promised Malika, "I will never lie to you again and I will never cheat on you again, unless it's your idea and we like the girl an awful lot." Malika accepted Sam's apology, and Sam's last radio appearance remained unbelievable right until the end.

seconds before he died.

Malika, although battered and suffering from a concussion, would be okay after a stay in the hospital. The seventeen-year-old driver of the pickup truck, who had been drinking, was charged with vehicular manslaughter and gross negligence, and ended up with a sentence of three hundred hours of com-

Sam with Malika and her sister Sabrina. (Vincent Zuffante/Star File)

munity service. Sam was buried in Tulsa, Oklahoma, a few
days later.

The world had lost one of its funniest comedians, and
Howard had lost one of his best friends and favorite guests.
Howard remembered Sam in *Rolling Stone* as "a major talent
with a brilliant comic mind. Sam's bad night was a lot more
interesting than just about anyone else's best night." Howard
also stated, " . . . he was utterly real. I think if Sam had fucked
his own sister, he would have called me on the air the very next
day to talk about it. And he would have made it funny, too. That
sort of honesty got Sam in trouble, but it was also what made
him incredible to listen to." You almost get the feeling that
Howard is describing himself when he talks about Sam.

Howard put together a Sam Kinison tribute show on the

radio and dedicated an episode of the WWOR TV show "to my friend, Sam Kinison." The radio show was a tearjerker, containing one of the most touching tribute songs you will ever hear. It was called "The Sounds of Kinison" and was sung by Fred Norris to the tune of "The Sounds of Silence." Lines such as "Good-bye, Kinison, my old friend; it's sad that car crash was your end" were intermixed with clips from live Sam appearances. The rest of the show was dedicated to playing the best Sam clips from the Stern show, although there were too many to squeeze into the four-and-a-half-hour broadcast. Ironically enough, Sam was booked to call Howard on that Monday's radio show.

Howard ended his tribute to Sam by playing "The Sounds of Kinison" once more, followed by Sam's great hit song, "Wild Thing" and then "Funeral for a Friend." It was a great tribute from one good friend to another. Fittingly, Howard's listeners were also allowed to pay their last respects, along with Howard, to the greatest of all Stern guests.

Finally, some last words from Sam's onetime lover, fellow religious dropout, and fellow Stern worshiper, Jessica Hahn: "He hated religion, but he was definitely a man who loved God. He had a cross inside the lining of that long coat he used to wear. It was no joke to him." Jessica was also quoted as saying that she had spoken to Sam a few weeks before he died and was once again becoming friends with him. "He sounded like a new person. Now he's in God's arms. I know the last second of his life was peaceful."

Sam, you brought some great moments to the *Howard Stern Show*. Even when you set us up, it was the greatest radio we were ever going to hear. We couldn't wait for the reunion between Howard and yourself and we were thrilled every time you made an appearance. You were and always will be the best Stern guest ever. We miss your laugh, your message, and your scream. Sam Kinison: 1953–1992.

CHAPTER

8

TELEVISION: FROM FOX TO E!

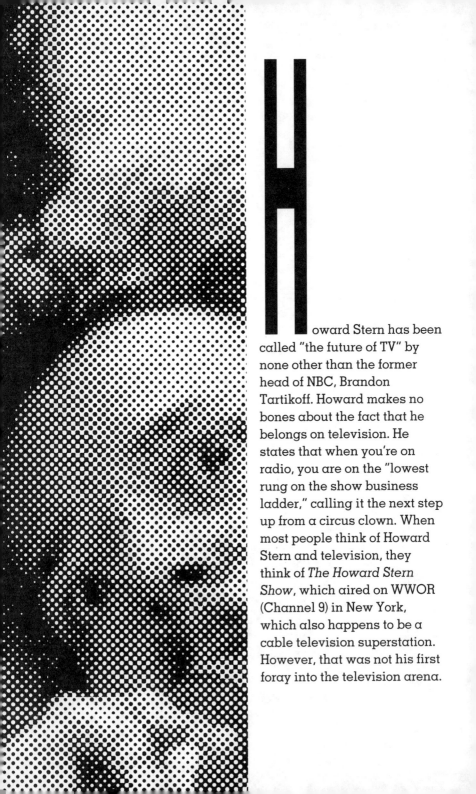

Howard Stern has been called "the future of TV" by none other than the former head of NBC, Brandon Tartikoff. Howard makes no bones about the fact that he belongs on television. He states that when you're on radio, you are on the "lowest rung on the show business ladder," calling it the next step up from a circus clown. When most people think of Howard Stern and television, they think of *The Howard Stern Show*, which aired on WWOR (Channel 9) in New York, which also happens to be a cable television superstation. However, that was not his first foray into the television arena.

In 1985, Howard Stern was hired by the Fox network to create a talk show. The show was going to be the replacement for *The Joan Rivers Show*, which was receiving bad ratings. Unfortunately for Howard, creative control of the show was taken out of Howard's hands and instead given to a group of writers Fox had hired. They turned it into just another of the numerous talk shows you see nowadays. Predictably, Howard was unhappy from the start, and the show was never picked up by Fox.

In retaliation, Howard went on talk shows, including Fox's own *Late Night Show*, hosted by Arsenio Hall, and told audiences that Fox was responsible for the death of Edgar Rosenberg, Joan Rivers's husband, who committed suicide at the time when Joan's Fox show was floundering. Howard still has not forgiven Fox and trashes them weekly, if not more often.

Howard's next attempt at television was much more successful, and it was because this time he made sure he had creative control over the show. *The Howard Stern Show*, which began airing on WWOR in 1990 and lasted for two years, has to be the most daring, innovative, and funny show ever broadcast over the television airwaves. The show was picked up in fifty-two cities, usually extremely late at night due to the risqué bits Howard would air. The show would often beat *Saturday Night Live* in the ratings in the New York market. This was unprecedented, and quite a feat for a low-budget show aired on an independent station out of Secaucus, New Jersey.

The Howard Stern Show was, in essence, a visual presentation of his radio show. He was able to bring along all of his team from the radio show, including, of course, cohost Robin Quivers. He also brought along the news, his commentary, his live pitches for Snapple and other products, and celebrity guests, both regulars from the radio show and new guests like Bob Hope. This was the absolute cutting edge of television.

The TV show opened some creative avenues for Howard to pursue that were not a possibility when he was broadcasting strictly over the radio. The most obvious examples of this were the television game show spoofs that Howard pulled off on an almost weekly basis. The first one, "Lesbian Dating Game," started out as an offshoot of "Lesbian Dial-a-Date" from the radio show, but Howard soon branched out to give us such classics as "Homeless Howiewood Squares," "Hooker Price Is Right," "Crown Heights Jeopardy," and even "You Bet Your Ass." Gene Rayburn, the host of the highly successful *Match Game* from the '70s, once told Howard that no one had ever been successful at doing a game show parody. That was before Howard came along and turned it into an art form.

Let's review the keys to a successful game show parody. First, make sure the contestants are people that Bob Barker and Chuck Woolery would never consider having appear on their game shows, such as hookers, lesbians, homeless people, swingers, or anyone else who does not look like the average Joe. Next, add a host who is a comedic genius with a biting sense of humor. Finally, throw in an occasional celebrity and/or person with a cause, such as the "KKK Guy," and you've got yourself a fine game show parody.

Lesbians, lesbians, lesbians!!! Lesbians were definitely Howard's favorite people to use when spoofing a game show.

The "Lesbian Dating Game" introduced us to "Becky," the tattooed biker chick with a ring in her nose. "Becky" would turn this small slice of exposure into regular appearances on Howard's show. She probably ended up getting more babes from her stints on the Stern show than any other guest, male or female. Now *there* is one lesbian who does not find Howard to be offensive toward women. Good thing for Howard, as she looked like she could kick his ass in just under three seconds.

The "Lesbian Dating Game" was hosted by "Howard Lang." During the second "Dating Game," Howard told the three contestants, "If I kissed you, you all would change. . . . Maybe not you, Number Two," directing this remark to a particularly masculine-looking lesbian. Howard gives us a pretty clear hint at the end of that segment why we got to see so many lesbians on his show. "I love it when two girls get together. . . . I think it's the biggest turn-on in the world. God bless you lesbians!"

During "Lesbian Love Connection," featuring "Becky" and a young, gorgeous married lady called "Michelle," the girls were grilled by none other than "Chuck Wollybush." After learning from Michelle that Becky did indeed come over to Michelle's house for the date, Chuck said, "Let's meet the woman of your hot, moist dreams." He also asked: "Michelle, what would I smell on your breath?" We learn that in fact the two ladies did have sex, while Michelle's husband watched. When asked to describe Becky's tongue, Michelle replied, "Way cool." The show ended with Chuck noting, "I think they all need a tube of toothpaste."

My personal favorite bit with a lesbian occurred during a spoof of *What's My Line* called "What's My Secret." This routine included having Kitty Carlisle Hart and Arlene Francis appear as panelists. These are the two ladies who used to appear on the old *What's My Line* game show as regulars. It was amazing to me that Howard could possibly talk the two of them into appearing on his show.

"Heather," a shapely blonde in a bikini, was introduced as a "former Miss New York State, Miss Tri-State, and Miss Hemisphere," and the panel, which included Robin, had to guess her secret. The spoof began with a memorable exchange between Howard and Arlene Francis. Howard opened, "I will begin the questioning with Arlene Francis, or should I say Miss Francis. For me to even call you Arlene would be completely out of the question. Would it not, Miss Francis?" Miss Francis responded, "I would like you to call me whatever gives you pleasure." To which Howard replied, "Well then, it would be My Sweet Little Love Potato. . . . " This got even Miss Francis to crack a smile.

Anyway, the show ran much in the same way an old episode of *What's My Line* would have, with the panelists asking questions of Heather in trying to guess her secret. Of course, they did not guess it, and Howard had to reveal to them that Heather's secret was that she is a lesbian. Both Arlene Francis and Kitty Carlisle Hart seemed stunned by this revelation. You could almost see the regret spelled out on their faces over ever having agreed to do the show.

After the bit ended, Howard asked Arlene, who once had a long-running radio show on WOR, the following: "I'm sure as a fellow broadcaster you support me in my efforts against the government. Am I correct?" Arlene Francis, who now looked totally annoyed, did not even answer him. This was a classic piece of television.

Lesbians even play a part in some of the game show spoofs they are not featured in. "Homeless Howiewood Squares" featured a Lesbian Square as the Stern show's "ratings insurance." This was one of the funnier parodies on the show, as it had two semicoherent homeless females vying against two semicoherent homeless males for a chance at the grand prize, a shopping cart filled with aluminum cans plus an unspecified amount of money. The contestants who picked the secret square would win "a new home," which was a cardboard refrigerator box. Besides the Lesbian Square, there were squares occupied by Gene Rayburn, Jaye P. Morgan, the "KKK Guy," Teresa Glover (a black woman who sat in the square next to the KKK Guy), "Underdog Lady," David Peel (a pot proponent who produced an album with John Lennon), Vinnie D'Amico (whose claim to fame is eating live worms and banging pots on his head), and (Martha Raye's husband) Mark Harris, who was introduced as "a man with a love for dentures and Depends diapers, Mr. Martha Raye." Yes, this was the Squares from Hell.

Howard, at his hosting best, started out by supplying us with a detailed description of how to play the game: "The rules are, it's freakin tic-tac-toe." The questions, much in the manner of the real *Hollywood Squares*, were geared toward each particular square. The KKK Guy's first question was, "What year was Martin Luther King assassinated?" Gene Rayburn was asked to fill in the blank in a *Match Game* scenario, *blank*-a-doodle-doo.

The homeless men were having a tough time with this one, so Howard leaned over and whispered the answer to one of them. Unfortunately, he misheard Howard and answered "pog." Gene went with the more traditional answer, "cock," which gave Howard the opportunity to push those television boundaries by announcing, "Gene has 'cock.'" (Incidentally, Jaye P. Morgan's answer was, "Spank-my-doodle-doo.")

Mark Harris, a younger gentleman who married seventy-five-year old Martha Raye and whom Howard picks on as possibly being gay, was asked, "What condition causes the vaginal walls to get thinner and the vulva to atrophy?" The answer, of course, was "old age."

The best exchanges were between Howard and Underdog Lady, otherwise known as Suzanne Muldowney. This is a lady who likes to seriously portray Underdog, the cartoon character, through interpretive dance. (Where in the hell does Howard find these people?) The Underdog Lady and the KKK Guy were my two favorite regular guests on the TV show. I think it is because both of them took their "jobs" so seriously while being at the same time so out of touch with reality.

I'm sorry, but as hateful, racist, and ignorant as the KKK Guy is, I couldn't help but feel sorry for him when the rest of the squares ganged up on him. However, I'm sure I would feel different if I was Teresa, the KKK Guys' neighbor on the show; she had to put up with "nigger" references throughout the show. But she didn't have a lot of trouble putting the KKK Guy in his place. "Every time you say nigger, you disgrace your mama," she told the KKK Guy after one particularly nasty exchange.

Anyway, where else on television would you be able to see a proud black woman and a member of the KKK play a game together? Leave it to Howard to try and promote racial harmony through tic-tac-toe.

Let's get back to Underdog Lady. The first question ever asked of her during "Homeless Howiewood Squares" was, "Is it possible for Underdog, or any dog in the animal kingdom, to practice homosexuality?" Underdog Lady was extremely upset by this question and loudly answered, "*No!* He is never depicted as doing that, and that is another example of an adult vice that a superhero is not allowed to show in order to set a good example for the viewers."

"Homeless Howiewood Squares" was won by the homeless men, who picked Teresa as their "lucky square." Her key unlocked the shopping cart and everyone lived happily ever after, except those viewers at home who felt it necessary to feel offended on behalf of homeless people everywhere. These viewers ended up being represented by one "Ann Julian" of Boston during another parody.

"Stern's People's Court" was an important spoof, because for once Howard got a chance to answer all those people out there who feel he mocks the homeless, the handicapped, ethnic groups, lesbians, or any other group represented by someone that Howard has on. Well, Ann from Boston was mad at Howard for "mocking the homeless," and she was going to have her say on TV in front of a genuine practicing attorney who would act as the judge.

Ann called Howard "disgusting and cruel" and was upset about his offering the homeless contestants a cardboard box and a shopping cart full of cans as prizes. She also stated that it "broke a lot of people's hearts" to see that one of the homeless contestants appeared to be mentally retarded.

I can't say what motivated Ann to appear on Howard's show, but I do feel that there are a lot of people who want to keep the homeless, the handicapped, and anyone else who is a bit different from themselves out of the public eye and in a closet somewhere. This way they don't have to deal with them at all. Howard sort of said it all in his closing statement: "Every game show is sanitized with perfect people playing perfect games. . . . Should a homeless person be deprived of going on a game show and winning money too?"

Ann, as Howard suggested, should direct her wrath at mainstream game shows like *Jeopardy!* and *The Price Is Right* that never even acknowledge the existence of the homeless. I, for one, was glad to hear Howard's assurances that he would never ban the homeless or any other group from appearing on his show.

Why do some people have such a hard time understanding that someone like Howard Stern, who picks on and has fun with every group and everyone, including himself, is not the problem in society? Howard is giving exposure to people and groups that no one else on TV will accept. It is incredible that there are lesbians who are mad at Howard for "Lesbian Dating Game" and "Lesbian Love Connection." Shouldn't they instead be mad at the rest of the television world for not having any gay or lesbian programs on TV? Why get mad at the one person who is treating you as an equal?

I guess "Homeless Howiewood Squares" did not offend enough people, because Howard followed it up with "Hooker Howiewood Squares." Hookers rate second only to lesbians when it comes to Howard's game show spoofs, and this was one of his best hooker offerings. First of all, who else but the most outrageous personality in all of TV and radio would pit "Cindy Brady" (Susan Olsen) against "Bobby Brady" (Mike Lookinland) in a game of "Hooker Howiewood Squares." These were no fake hookers, either. There were the transvestites "Peaches and Shakila," at $40 each; she-males "Silver and Exotica," at $150 each; and "Jim and Jane Madam." There was also "Barbie," who, if you wanted her "B-side," would cost you $250. How about transsexual "Daisy Do It" who would "pack your meat for only twenty-five dollars." There was also "$60 Red"; "Kathy"—from the corner of 48th Street and 10th Avenue; "Mistress Victoria and Slave"; and the traditional "ratings insurance" Lesbian Square.

Cindy and Bobby both seemed to have a very good time with the show, especially Cindy. I'm not sure if he had actually died yet, but if he had, Mike Brady (Robert Reed) must have been rolling over in his grave. (Well, maybe not, considering the secret life Mr. Brady had been hiding all those years.) Anyway, Cindy and Bobby did not seem to have too much of a problem with questions like, "How many calories are there in a single sperm ejaculation of an average male?" (It's only five calories, for those of you playing at home who are trying to watch your weight.) Or how about this one: "According to Kinsey, out of every ten women, how many have had anal intercourse?" This question led Howard to deadpan, "Sherwood Schwartz [the creator of *The Brady Bunch*] did not write this show tonight." (Again for those of you playing at home, "Between three and four" was the answer.)

One of the funnier answers from a square came from "Kathy," who was asked, "How long does it take for the average woman to reach orgasm?" Her reply: "Three to five hours." I believe at least one of the hookers has had just a little too much sex. (The answer was eleven minutes.)

Cindy ended up outsmarting her television stepbrother, and proving she had a great sense of humor in the process. When Howard asked her if she lost her virginity to "your dad on *The Brady Bunch*," she answered, "No, it was another cast member. No, I'm kidding. Tiger [the Brady family dog]."

Well, there is no better game show to tie in with hookers than *The Price Is Right*. Wouldn't it be great if just once Bob Barker brought out a hooker and had his middle-American contestants guess how much she cost? Howard obviously wanted to see this, and created *The Hooker Price Is Right*, with your host, Bob Porker."

This show was set up in the same manner as the regular *Price Is Right*, except that there were three men bidding at the same time and one of them was Fred "Rerun" Berry from the old TV series *What's Happening!!* The first hooker was "Iris," a "twenty-five-year-old streetwalker with 38-double-D breasts." Iris was a rather large woman, so large that Howard asked her, "do you charge by the pound?" The contestants placed their bids on "straight sex" with Iris, and the winner, with a bid of $150.59, was Fred Berry. As an added prize, Fred got to play a game of trying to add up the prices of sex toys so they equaled more than $50. Fred picked a blowup doll, ben-wa balls, and a vibrator, for a winning total price tag of $59.

The next hooker was "Ms. B," who was thirty-five years old and had been a streetwalker since she was thirteen. This time the contestants had to bid on the question, "How much is it to use all three of Ms. B's inputs?" Ms. B was not a particularly attractive woman, so one of the contestants bid $5. This did not go over well with Ms. B. The actual cost was $100, which some would say was a bargain; but don't make that judgment until you have seen Ms. B. The "Showcase Showdown" had Fred and Mike bidding on a showcase that included dinner with Iris, porno videos, a limo, sexy lingerie, and a tube of K-Y jelly. Fred's bid was closer at $550, but because he went over, Mike won the *big* (sorry, Iris) prize.

Of course, if these shows were not your cup of tea, there was always "Hooker Family Feud," or "The Female Feud," as it was otherwise known. This game show spoof featured Howard dressed as a pimp, with categories such as "Place You Shave or Wax" and "Horniest Ethnic Group" (Japanese, followed by blacks, Italians, and Puerto Ricans, according to the Stern Survey).

Or how about "The $20 Pyramid," hosted by "Dick Stern," with celebrity guests Chuck Norris and Shadoe Stevens? Chuck's partner was a bikini-clad babe, while poor Shadoe ended up with Kenneth Keith Kallenbach, who made numerous appearances on the show, most of which involved attempts to blow smoke out of his eyes. Unbelievably, as many times as he tried this trick, he never quite mastered it. As a matter of fact, he would normally end up puking after his attempts, which was very appealing. Jeez, postal workers are usually so normal.

The two categories on "The $20 Pyramid" were "Sweater Meats" and "Sexual Aids." Chuck and partner chose the latter and ended up getting vibrator and porno movie but had trouble with K-Y jelly, ben-wa balls, liquor, and gerbil. Shadoe and Kenneth ended up with "Sweater Meats" and, scoring at home, I had them getting cans and knockers while missing jugs, hooters, boobs, and melons.

If my scoring was correct, we should have had a tie-breaker round, but Howard awarded the game to Chuck and the bikini girl, in what could have been one of the biggest game show scandals since the *$64,000 Question* fiasco in the 1950s. The finale, in which Chuck and his partner went for the big $20, proved to me that martial arts masters have no business being in the game show arena. Chuck could not get the hang of giving the clues to such categories as "Places You Masturbate," "Disgusting Things Humans Do," "Things Pee Wee Would Say to the Police," and "Obese Black Women."

Kenneth Keith Kallenbach showed up on another of the Stern game show bits. This time it was "The Couldn't Get Into College Bowl." The inspiration for this game was not Kenneth, but another brain surgeon, Sandi Korn, a finalist for *Penthouse* Pet of the Year, because she did not know which political party President Bush belonged to. She guessed Democrat. So Howard pitted the "occasional sex partner of Donald Trump" against Kenneth Keith Kallenbach and a seventh-grader.

Sandi, to her credit, did know how many days there are in a year and what Mrs. Bush's first name was. However, she did not know which country the United States declared its independence from, what ESP stands for, or who built the pyramids. I think this one question summed up the whole game: "What substance [do] diamonds come from?" Sandi answered "rock." Kenneth answered, "They're a substance by itself." The seventh-grade kid, of course, answered "coal."

"Queen for Today" was a show in which former child stars vied for the title of "Queen" by seeing who could tell the biggest sob story regarding their lives, while Howard "sobbed" into a washrag, then squeezed out his "tears" on the rug. The contestants were Erin Moran, who played "Joanie" on *Happy Days*; Billy Gray, who was "Bud" on *Father Knows Best*; and Lauren Chapin, who was "Kitten" on the same show. Erin went first and told how she was not a happy child star, as she was "abused by the Hollywood system." Billy Gray's story was a bit sadder: He was arrested and thrown in jail for possession of marijuana at the age of twenty, and no one came to bail him out. He never acted after that and claims the producers of the show ripped him off for $80,000.

But neither of the above was any match for Kitten. She started by saying she had been sexually abused by her father. (Howard, of course realizing what an emotional moment it was, stated, "At home it was 'Father Knows Daughter' and on the set it was *Father Knows Best.*) This was only the beginning. Her boyfriend beat her up. She did heroin for eight years. She went to jail for forging a check to pay for her heroin. (Again, the compassionate Howard shone through; "Kitten in prison; I love prison lesbian stories.") She spent three years in jail and tried to commit suicide with a meat cleaver, and she spent another year and a half in a mental institution. Poor Kitten!

As if he needed to, Howard held his hands over the contestants' heads to have the audience vote for the saddest story on the applaud-o-meter. As he raised his hands over Erin's head, he casually asked, "Were you ever raped?" Very unexpectedly, Erin answered, "Yes," then went on to say she was raped by "a family member" when she was twenty-three. Howard asked, "You're not just saying this to get points? You're being serious?" She was being serious. Howard then moved on to Billy Gray. "Now, Billy, do you want to say you were raped by Robert Young?" he asked. At this point Erin lost her composure and broke down. Howard did his best to make her feel better, giving her a hug, and it seemed to work.

I'm not sure what would possess someone to choose *The Howard Stern Show* to reveal for the first time ever that she had been raped; but that is just what Erin did. Somehow, Howard has a way of getting people to reveal their deepest secrets to him.

In any case, despite Erin's sudden disclosure, she still could not take the "Queen for Today" crown away from Lauren Chapin. Let's face it, Helen Keller would have had a tough time wrestling the crown away from Lauren after the sad story she told.

There were some TV bits that WWOR found just too darn offensive to air in their entirety. These included "Black Jeopardy," which contained categories like "Fat Blacks" and "Black Spelling." But probably the game show that would have garnered the most complaints if it had aired would have been "Handicapped Beat the Clock." This spoof pitted a one-legged guy against a man in a wheelchair as they competed in various obstacle courses.

There was one game show spoof that Howard *didn't* host; instead, he was a contestant. "The Sternlywed Game" pitted Howard and Alison against Fred Norris and his better half, also Alison (aka Princess Norris); Stuttering John and his girlfriend, Karen; and producer Dan Forman and his wife, Robin. We get some great inside information on the personal lives of all four couples. Both Alison and Howard agreed that the first thing he does after "making whoopee" is "roll over and go to sleep." We also found out that Howard's penis is not as small as he leads everyone to believe. Both he and his wife answered "six inches" to a question dealing with penis length. Stuttering John and his girlfriend also agreed that his penis was six inches long, while Fred said his was six and a half inches while his spouse answered seven. Fred, for God's sake, man, round up!! The funniest answer was Dan Forman's, who answered seven inches while Robin answered five. Grounds for instant divorce? You be the judge!

Another classic moment during the game was provided by Stuttering John and his girlfriend. The question was "What is the single wildest thing [your mate has ever done]?" John's answer was "She masturbated for me." Karen was stunned by his answer and screamed, "Oh my God, that is not true" and later, "Oh my God, get me off this show." The funny thing is, *her* answer was "Oral sex at a gig." Oral sex is okay to admit to, but masturbation is not? Howard's answer to the same question was "We had sex on the floor," while Alison's was "Making love in a sink." Both answers ended up being unsatisfactory to Howard, who told Alison, "Why can't you be like Karen over there?" For you Fred Norris fans, his answer was "On beach in St. Bart's," while his Alison answered, "Slept with him on first date," to which Howard commented, "Slut."

The bonus question was "Most number of times you made whoopee in one session?" John and Karen both answered five, for a match. Our long-haired, speech-impaired interviewer is quite the Casanova. Fred answered five and Alison three. Maybe that was with someone else, Fred. Dan Foreman and

Robin both answered two, which would have been pretty funny, except for the fact that Howard and Alison both answered *one!!* One?? You have got to be kidding. Remember, these two met in college. With that answer, Howard and Alison actually won the game, but Howard stated, "I don't know what I'm cheering about, I'm pretty depressed." One. Jeez, Howard—Dan Forman's done it *twice!*

Howard is a people person. He loves to have ordinary people on his show who believe they possess some special talent. One of the earliest Stern shows featured not only Kenneth Keith Kallenbach and his first attempt to blow smoke through his eyes, but a man who put a chain in his nose and pulled it out through his mouth. And as if that wasn't enough talent for one episode, we also got to see a man who could let his saliva drool into a bowl of popcorn, only to suck it back up into his mouth with a kernel of popcorn attached like some perverse frog. I bet you Orville Redenbacher couldn't do that.

In another episode, titled "Howard Stern Talks to His Audience," we got a chance to meet average viewers who for some reason believe they have a talent the rest of us would like to see.

The rules for speaking to Howard were as follows:

1● "Do not look Howard directly in the eyes."

2● "Howard will be referred to at all times as Mr. Stern."

3● "No chewing gum."

4● "Do not touch your genital areas at any time."

The many viewers who had the great honor of being able to speak to Mr. Stern had a variety of talents and/or problems. One guy drove a four-inch nail up his nose; a spokesmodel ate a lobster, shell and all; and one guy could make fart noises using all of the joints of his body.

The most important guest to show up this particular evening was Susan Muldowney, whom I have already introduced to everyone as the Underdog Lady. It was here that the

TEN STRANGEST GUESTS WHO EVER APPEARED ON THE HOWARD STERN SHOW ON WWOR

● 1 ●

The KKK Guy

● 2 ●

Underdog Lady

● 3 ●

Kenneth Keith Kallenbach

● 4 ●

The Kielbasa Queen

● 5 ●

"Becky the Biker Lesbian"

● 6 ●

Tula, a transsexual

● 7 ●

Vinnie D'Amico, who ate a plate of live earthworms

● 8 ●

Mark Harris, the extremely effeminate,
much younger husband of Martha Raye

● 9 ●

"Fred the Elephant Boy"

● 10 ●

Silver and Exotica,
"she-males"

Underdog Lady made her *Howard Stern Show* debut actually doing the "Underdog Dance" for us. Afterward, Howard told her, "I only wish for you that one day you meet a man and have a husband and that he performs a Snagglepuss."

After a totally incoherent guest or two, we got to the most disgusting act of the evening, the guy "who will eat anything." This guy had Gary chew up a Twinkie and spit it out, then retrieved and ate it. He'd told Howard beforehand that it was hardly a challenge. Well, my goodness, why not have the guy wait until Gary digests the Twinkie next time?

Finally, if we were not sure about the other guests needing some kind of psychiatric help, we had no doubt about the last one. This guy is obsessive about the number four. He has to rip off four pieces of toilet paper, then wipe four times. Hey, good thing he's not obsessed with the number one, or he'd be ruining quite a few pairs of underwear, wouldn't he?

Let's take a moment now to review what we have learned about Howard. He is not only an advocate of special interest groups like the homeless, handicapped, lesbian, and stupid, but he is also an advocate of the common man. (Can anyone honestly tell me that the man who sucked up a piece of popcorn with his own drool was going to find a forum for his skill any-where else on TV?) There is one other group that Howard is cer-tainly an advocate for, and there is nothing common about this group. Yes, I am talking about the well-endowed female.

This is also what gets Howard into trouble with all of the feminist organizations in the world. The National Organization for Women, led by Tammy Bruce, announced plans to boycott Simon & Schuster for the publication of Howard's book, *Private Parts*. The boycott has really hurt sales of *Private Parts*, as it took Howard a full month to have over 1 million copies of his book in print.

(By the way, Howard's original title for his book was reject-ed by Simon & Schuster; he wanted it called *Mein Kampf*. I guess Simon didn't want it confused with any other books by this title.)

STERN'S EXPOSES HIS "PRIVATE PARTS" TO THE LITERARY WORLD

Howard's autobiography, *Private Parts*, surprised everyone in the publishing industry. The book instantly became the bestselling title in the entire country and jumped to the number one spots on the *New York Times*, *Publishers Weekly*, *USA Today*, and everyone else's bestseller list. During a Stern appearance on *Late Show*, David Letterman told his audience that *Private Parts* was the "fastest-selling publication in the seventy-year history of Simon & Schuster." At two book signings in Manhattan, Howard saw a total of over 25,000 fans show up, and streets in New York had to be closed off. He had the same type of turnout for a signing in Philadelphia. Howard really has proven to be "King of All Media," as he likes to refer to himself.

NOW had also threatened to boycott the E! Channel because it had hired Howard to do his interview show. To appease NOW and Ms. Bruce, E! offered a series called, "Women on the Verge: Breaking Media Myths." Well, I'm sure that will garner some big ratings.

I can tell you, Ms. Bruce, that when Diane Welsh, who was president of the New York City chapter of NOW, appeared on *The Howard Stern Show* during the swimsuit episode, she did not seem to have a lot of bad things to say about Howard or the show. As a matter of fact, she stated, "I appreciate that, like feminism, you are pushing the envelope of what's acceptable in society." Thank you, Diane, you are absolutely correct, and I can't help but wonder if you have been thrown out of NOW because since your appearance on the show, the organization seems to be totally out of control.

Okay, Diane didn't agree with Howard on all things; But tell me, why is it that the females who pose for these magazines or the females who appear on *The Howard Stern Show* as spokesmodels don't seem to have a problem with men looking at them? Is NOW saying that all of these females are stupid? Diane urged us at the end of her appearance on the Stern show to "at least try, just this once, to see women as a whole being." Or did she mean "hole being"? Lighten up, I was just kidding!

The swimsuit episode was a show in which Howard had girls compete with one another to become his "cover model." The finalists included Puerto Rican twins to whom Howard commented, "You stole the same bathing suits, didn't you"; a chemical engineer from Princeton University (she doesn't seem too stupid, does she NOW?), who also has a brown belt in judo and flipped Boy Gary just to prove it; and African-American girl who when she bent over for Howard, had to have her crotch blacked out; and finally, a twenty-three-year-old who told Howard, "I'm saving myself for you," and who was the only girl who took off her top for Howard just to get into the finals.

The finals consisted solely of the girls modeling their wares. "Barbi," the judo girl, rubbed oil on herself. "Millie and

Lilly," the twins, posed in a bathroom setting, complete with erotic posing accompanied by a plunger, while Jackie Martling was in the next stall taking a dump. This was quite a disadvantage to the twins, and prompted Howard to ask, "Hey, Jackie, how about a courtesy flush over there?" "Eschelle," Howard's "African Queen," was asked to model with a black guy in a grass skirt posing as a wild African native. They were joined by Kessler, the black dwarf who appeared regularly on the show, pulling Stuttering John around by a chain as he did his "Cornelius" (of *Planet of the Apes*) impression. Howard noted that the set was beginning to look like "*The Jeffersons* in hell."

"Devon," the twenty-three-year-old vixen, was the girl who struck the best poses and was the only one willing to take her top off, so she won and become the "cover model."

With the Stern show you did not have to wait until a special swimsuit episode to see beautiful, bodacious babes; they were a weekly happening, because Howard is a believer in the "spokesmodel." Actually, Howard is a believer in ratings, and the spokesmodels were ratings grabbers and at the same time a great way to sell Snapple and other products.

Howard's spokesmodels included the likes of "Busty Dusty," "Dixie Dynamite," and "Chesty Love," among others. These were the spokesmodels who had breasts the size of watermelons or larger. He also had the *Penthouse* and *Playboy* caliber of spokesmodel, such as Amy Lynn and Sandi Korn. He even had a pregnant spokesmodel. However, most of them were just good-looking women who were regular people who wanted to appear as spokesmodels on *The Howard Stern Show*. They were the same type of women who tried out for the honor of being the first and only annual "Spokesmodel of the Year."

This was probably the best takeoff on the "Miss America" contest you will ever see. It grabbed your attention right from the opening number, sung to the tune of "That's Entertainment," in which all of the girls in the competition sang lines like, "We're cute and our hooters are firm; we love Howard, though he's hung like a worm." The introduction of the contestants included their names and breast sizes. The girls were going to be judged on "talent," "modeling," and "personality" by celebrity judges Lloyd Lindsay Young, a WWOR weatherman; Mason Reese, a former child television commercial star; and Tula, a woman who was once a man.

The contestants showed that they really were a talented group. Their talents included reading a book, balancing a bowl of fruit on the head, blowing bubbles, doing jumping jacks, chewing gum, and eating cherries with whipped cream. The girl who probably showed the most talent was the one who did a split, prompting Howard to exclaim, "Whoa, she stuck to the floor, Robin." Before the winner was announced, Howard offered $500 to any of the finalists willing to take off her top. As fate would have it, the only contestant willing to take off her top, "Veronica," was also the contestant chosen to be "Spokesmodel of the Year—1991." Veronica will live on as Spokesmodel of Eternity, as Howard never had a chance to run the contest again before WWOR pulled the plug on his show.

Luckily for everyone, WWOR could not accomplish it's devil's work before Howard had the chance to do his "Tribute to Breasts" show. This show also went under the names of "Tribute to Lung Lumps," "Sweater Meat," "Chest Chubbies," "Dirty Pillows," "Lacto Monsters," "Milk Wagons," "Bubbie Wubbies," and "Sag Bags." It truly was a special episode—and wasn't it about time that someone acknowledged the contributions that breasts have made to society. Again, thank God for Howard Stern.

Some of the more memorable moments from the show include a Stuttering John interview to find out what the "man on the street" thinks about breasts. John tracked down a clown who was on the street rallying a protest against cruelty to circus animals (only in New York). After the clown told John what he was protesting against, John stated, "Ah, come on, nobody cares about that. What do you think about breasts? The clown got pissed off and walked away. What other show could actually piss off a clown?

And talk about a show that points out the hypocrisy in our society. Howard was not allowed to show us a "modern" white woman's breasts; however, he was allowed to show film of "native" African women naked from the waist up. Now here is a cause that damn sensitive clown should be taking up.

The finale to this show was a heart-wrencher. If you were moved by "We Are the World"' and "Feed the World" and the celebrities who pulled together to do those two benefit songs, then you certainly were impressed with Howard's efforts on behalf of breasts everywhere. He got together the likes of Michael Spinks, Mason Reese, the Ramones, Lloyd Lindsay Young, and Uncle Floyd—yes, all the big names in showbiz—for this special salute. (I guess Joe Franklin was busy.) With all of the aforementioned stars, as well as Robin, Jackie, Fred, Stuttering John, and some bikini-clad breast carriers, Howard pulled off an amazing musical tribute called, "Breasts Feed the World." As Howard stated, "You don't necessarily need to respect the woman attached to the breast, but respect the breasts themselves."

Some of the lyrics in this classic song, sung to the tune of "We Are the World," included "They're a wonderful gland and they fit inside your hand" and "In tight tops they make us mental—white, black or Oriental." Robin had her own solo verse in the song that included the line, "They are the place you'll find my boyfriend's face." Wow; it just sort of makes you want to bury your head between a nice set of hooters and have a good cry.

Nothing was sacred on *The Howard Stern Show*, not Jesus, not Santa Claus, and not even the King himself. No, not you, Howard; this time I'm referring to Elvis. Howard had a running bit on his radio show in which he would call up the spirit of Elvis to come and speak through him. But I think Elvis saved his best appearance for the TV show. That particular episode aired soon after a *National Enquirer* article claimed that Elvis and his mother were lovers. Of course, Elvis wanted to take over Howard's body so he could talk over these serious allegations with a disturbed nation.

JESSICA HAHN AND HER "HANGING FRIENDS"

Jessica Hahn
helped Howard celebrate
the breast by answering some
poignant questions on the subject.
Howard asked, "How do you care for
your hanging friends?" Jessica replied
that she "massaged them with oil," which
certainly got my imagination jump-started.
Howard also inquired, "Which breast was Jim
Bakker's favorite?" Jessica, not pleased with
this inquiry, responded, "That's not funny."
When Howard asked Jessica, "What's
the highest compliment your breasts
have ever received?" she replied,
"That they're so fluffy." Jessica,
I'm pretty sure I could top
that one, if you would
only call.

Jessica Hahn and her "hanging friends."

I think everyone was shocked when Elvis disclosed, "I admit it, I done slept with my pig of a mother. It started at a very young age. First my mama played with herself while she watched me take a dump." Elvis even went as far as rewriting the lyrics to his hit "Hound Dog" as a "tribute" to his mama. "She ain't nothing but a big hog, but I humped her all the time . . . " he sang.

It wasn't too long after this appearance by Elvis that Howard ran one of his commercial spoofs asking viewers to call in and vote for their favorite Elvis stamp. Your choices, in case you missed it, were either the "bloated, overeating Elvis" or the "incestuous, horny Elvis." Of course, this was just one of those 900 scams, as you had to dial "900-Big Dead Slob" or "900-Mama Lover" to place your vote. Actually, I'm pretty sure there are a lot of Elvis freaks out there who wouldn't mind licking the "incestuous, horny Elvis" (stamp, that is).

Other memorable episodes of the Stern TV show, which ran for two and a half years, include the two "House Party" broadcasts. These were shows in which Howard left the safe confines of the studio in favor of some viewer's residence. One house was on the verge of being repossessed by the bank, so the owners were pretty much using the television opportunity to destroy it. They had some pretty unique ways of accomplishing this, such as having three babes roll in paint and throw themselves up against a nice white wall, which made for some unusual avant garde artwork.

Other fun games included a "Put-the-Condom-on-the-Banana Race," which was billed as a "public-service announcement" to encourage safe sex, and the "Hot Dog Game," where girls ate hot dogs dangled from guys' strings. This, of course, gave Howard the opportunity to ask one of the contestants, "Have you ever had anything in your mouth this long?" My favorite game that evening had to be "Bobbing for Tampons." Imagine just how proud the mayor of a small New Jersey shore town had to be when he heard that his son had won "Bobbing for Tampons" on nationwide television. It was amazing that with the thrill of victory, and the taste of tampons still in his mouth, this fine young man nonetheless had the good common sense to announce to the world who his father was.

I, along with millions of other Howard Stern fans, was crushed when I heard that WWOR was pulling the plug on this ground-breaking show. It is still not clear who was more responsible for the death of *The Howard Stern Show*, Howard himself or the management of WWOR. It was clear that there were some deep hostilities between Howard and the station. Howard would constantly bad-mouth WWOR on the air, and I'm sure management had to be a bit annoyed with its biggest star.

I think the episode that ran this message on the screen says it all abut the tensions which were growing between Howard and his television bosses: "In the final segment we wanted to show you an unbelievably funny Stuttering John interview with James Brown, but we ran a little late and WWOR threw us out of the studio. Hopefully, we will have a complete show next week."

This had to have been a total embarrassment to the big-wigs at WWOR. They had just been spanked in public, on their own airwaves, for an occurrence they should never have let happen in the first place. What kind of station kicks a crew out of a studio when they are trying to prepare that week's TV show?

What WWOR offered as an excuse for the cancellation of the show was that "production" costs were higher than the earnings that the show was generating, even though it was syndicated to fifty-three different markets. This is hard to believe, since this show was regularly beating *Saturday Night Live* in the New York market. On top of that, how much could the "production" costs have been? It looked like one of the cheapest shows on television.

Howard disagrees with WWOR's assessment as to why the show ended. He constantly griped over the show's poor production values. He has stated publicly that he left voluntarily to pursue other interests, such as a movie career: "How can I work there when I got Hollywood beckoning me?" He has said he was "furious" that WWOR claimed the show had been canceled.

Whatever the reason, it was a shame to see the show end. There may never be another like it. I think Howard summed up the program best when he said, "Our show isn't just about bare skin and big boobs; occasionally we sneak in a nice crotch shot too." Howard's new program on the E! cable channel is the best interview show going, but does not come close to equaling *The Howard Stern Show* for pure comedy entertainment.

I'm sure not everyone was saddened to learn that the show was coming to an end. There was the station in Naples, Florida, which had received complaints from the local Catholic church, and there was the lady who came on the show calling Howard a "chauvinistic pig,'" and the gentleman who was upset with Howard because his kids wanted to watch the show, he wouldn't allow them to, and they hated him for it.

Well, my response is that the Catholic Church should be more concerned with *60 Minutes* and its report about priests molesting children than with *The Howard Stern Show*. The lady who thinks Howard is a "chauvinistic pig" should have changed the television dial. And to that last guy: It's called parenting!

As Howard once stated, "For every ten thousand quacks out there who want to see me taken off the air, there are ten or twenty really sick shut-ins who worship my every movement." Ah, come on Howard, you have a lot more than ten or twenty really sick shut-ins who worship your every movement.

I said it before, and I'll say it gain: *The Howard Stern Interview* is the best talk show currently on TV.

Howard, in an interview he gave to *Entertainment Weekly* in October, stated that he would "consider it" if Fox offered him the deal. He has since stated on his radio show that he would be very interested in going up against Leno and Letterman. If the management at Fox has any brains at all, it would realize that Stern is the only personality out there right now who could actually take viewers away from both Letterman and Leno.

Unfortunately, it airs on a cable station that is not available in a lot of areas. Matthew Gilbert of the *Boston Globe* called Howard the "Arsenio antidote," which is about the best description I have ever heard. It pretty much means that Howard is not interviewing his guests just so he can kiss their butts, much like "Assmoochio" and others do. Howard did not

HOWARD WORK FOR FOX?

When Chevy Chase's show was abruptly removed from the airwaves in October of 1993 by the Fox network, there were many rumors floating around the industry about who would replace the incredibly inept Chase. One of the names that popped up was Howard Stern. *TV Guide* ran a poll, and Howard was the hands-down winner as the choice to take over late-night duties on Fox. A Fox spokesman, however, denied that Howard was in the running.

develop this skill simply for *The Howard Stern Interview*; he has been conducting the same type of interview on his radio show for over a decade. There are no secrets. If you come on the *Stern Interview* you must be ready for the sex, bathroom, and scandal questions. If the *National Enquirer* has run an article saying that you go both ways, you can bet that Howard is going to ask you about it.

I must admit that I have come to respect the guests who

are willing to be interviewed by Howard, on both his radio and TV shows. I really respect the ones who seem to enjoy themselves and who have a sense of humor about the curves that Howard might throw their way. Howard seems to respect this, too. These guests have included the likes of Donald Trump, Joan Rivers, Gary Shandling, Bon Jovi, and Grace Slick. As a matter of fact, Howard's guest list is most impressive, considering his interview style and the fact that he is seen on E! As Howard has stated, "It's so easy getting guests when you have three viewers." But, boy, have those three viewers seen some unique interviews!

Where else can you hear Donald Trump get asked about AIDS testing, or see songwriter Richard Marx get berated because he refuses to perform for Howard? Who else would ask a guest when they lost their virginity or have the nerve to play "Butt Bongo" on Grace Slick? When Gary Shandling was asked by Howard why he agreed to be the first guest ever to do *The Howard Stern Interview*, he answered that it was because he had never gone skydiving or bungee-cord jumping.

Howard Stern was made for TV; unfortunately, it is probably TV in the year 2010. The ABCs, CBSs, and NBCs of this world are just too damn conservative and happy with their schlock television. People are tired of the same sickeningly sweet shows that we have been seeing since the '50s. That is why any show that takes a bit of a risk and attacks society's sacred cows, as *The Simpsons* and *Roseanne* do, fare so well. Unfortunately, these shows are few and far between.

God, I wish there was one network executive who had balls big enough to give Howard a shot on a major network with the type of show he had at WWOR. Howard Stern was the perfect person to replace David Letterman on *Late Night*. He is the only person who could keep Letterman's audience and add to it. Unfortunately, Brandon Tartikoff is correct when he states that Howard Stern is the "future of television," but it's only because the people in charge are not brave enough to take the heat they would receive if they hired Howard today.

STUTTERING

JOHN

think it is time to properly introduce the most recent addition to the Stern gang. He is the speech-impaired, long-haired, brass-balled interviewer who goes by the name of Stuttering John. Twenty-seven-year-old John Melendez joined Howard at K-Rock in 1989 as an unpaid intern. He soon turned his role as staff gofer into a regular spot on the radio show as the interviewer of those celebrities who refuse to come on the radio show. Yes, John tracks down his targets at various celebrity functions and showbiz events, then hits them with the most outrageous questions they have ever been asked. John is not

Stuttering John attempts to interview Chastity Bono. That's half brother Elijah Blue behind her. (Vincent Zuffante/Star File)

even responsible for the creation of the questions that he asks of his victi . . . I mean, interviewees. No, except for the rare ad-lib (for which Howard usually berates him), the questions are written down for John by Howard, Jackie, and Fred, and yes, they are doozies. They included this gem, which John asked of the former first lady of the Philippines, Imelda Marcos: "If you pass gas at home in front of others, do you blame the family dog?" Or how about this one that John delivered to the rock group ZZ Top: "Does Sinéad O'Connor give you a boner?"

If John doesn't write the questions and did not invent the genre, you may be asking, Why is he worthy of his own chapter? No, it's not because of his unique stuttering delivery, or because it's fun to see the celebs' reactions to a stuttering interviewer. There are two reasons why John is worthy of the attention he receives. The first is his determination to get to the celebrity he is after. He has been known to run after vehicles containing the likes of Bruce Springsteen and Jerry Brown. The second and more important reason John is one of my favorite Stern gangsters is that he will not back down from asking a celebrity whatever questions has been written out for him, no matter the risk. (Loudmouthed bore Morton Downey Jr. physically attacked John after he asked, "Would your wife go and dance topless in clubs for the money, if you really needed it?" Downey had just filed for bankruptcy.) John never backs down.

Although John had been doing celebrity interviews for the radio show, it was not until the WWOR television show began that you were really able to appreciate John's talents. For it is only on TV that you can see how hard it is for John to get out a question like "Did you ever fart in the catcher's face?" to ex–Boston Red Sox slugger Ted Williams. It is also only on TV that you could appreciate the fact that Ted really lacks a sense of humor, as he replied, "What kind of goddamn question is that?" Another sensitive ex–baseball player is Jim Bouton, who was offended by the other standard baseball-player question that Stuttering John delivers with his own unique style: "Who do you think got hit in the chin with more balls, Rock Hudson or Yogi Berra?"

John Melendez grew up in Massapequa, New York, Jessica Hahn's old hometown, which is not too far from where Howard himself spent his childhood. He is the lead singer and guitar player in a band, Rubber Beaver, and was recently signed to a record contract. Despite this and the fact that John has become an integral part of the show, Howard has continued to lambaste the guy for having "no future." Howard has dubbed John both "King of Interns" and "Hero of the Stupid." At one point during the TV show, Howard had thought about replacing John with a fellow who had Tourette's Syndrome, an affliction that causes uncontrollable grunting and cursing. Howard offered viewers a chance to call in and vote whether or not to replace John with this guy. Luckily for us and John, his fans came through and gave John 66 percent of the vote. We've been getting great inter-

Stuttering John attempts to interview Cher. (Vincent Zuffante/Star File)

views ever since.

John has also been able to gain some national exposure through his interviews. During a press conference with Gennifer Flowers, held to announce that she had slept with then presidential candidate Bill Clinton, John asked her, "Did Governor Clinton use a condom?" He also got in, "Will you be sleeping with any other presidential candidates?" as well as "Was there ever a threesome?" John not only brought down the house at the stuffy press conference, but he became a story in himself. Newspapers, including *USA Today*, wrote about his "lewd" questions in the following day's paper.

The reaction from Gennifer and her attorney was that of pure disgust, as they threatened to end the press conference if they were asked any further "degrading" questions. Howard pointed out on his radio show that here is a woman who's holding a press conference because she "spread her legs," but she's offended about a condom question. What a joke!

Gennifer could have taken some good-sport lessons from gossip columnist Liz Smith, who handled with grace and dignity a very difficult question, "Why are you such a fat cow?" Rival Cindy Adams also made out quite well with an equally difficult question regarding her husband, the ancient comedian Joey Adams. "When was the last time Joey had a solid bowel movement?" John asked Ms. Adams. "That's very good. That's one of your better ones. You look like he did it on you," was her reply to the thick-skinned stutterer.

Phil Donahue is used to asking tough questions of his guests, but obviously he was not prepared for Stuttering John's "Do you pray that Oprah will eat until she explodes?" Phil would only reply, "That's not funny." Phil's controversial wife, Marlo Thomas, did not fare much better in her interview with the famed stutterer, who called her "Marla" during the entire interview. Marlo's biggest problem was that she was interviewed by John while she was walking with noted feminist Gloria Steinem. Gloria chose to interrupt all the questions that were being directed at Marlo, such as "What word for woman do you find most degrading—chick, bimbo, bitch, babe, slut, or whore?" As Marlo was actually pondering the question, Gloria jumped in and ruined what could have been an important decision on Marlo's part. My guess is she would have gone for "slut."

There is a whole group of stars who attempt to run away from John the moment they see him coming. They include Warren Beatty, who was asked "What's bigger, the Oscar or your penis?" while he was walking with Annette Bening at the Academy Awards. His reply: "That's a very, very good question." He was gone by the time John asked him, "Do you remember sleeping with Joan Collins?" (John asked this question as he was getting knocked into some bushes by one of the people in Beatty's entourage.)

Larry King was running in circles in his own building

(Howard even retraced his confused path as a building floor plan) trying to get away from John and questions like "Why couldn't you get it up for Marilyn Chambers?" Cher couldn't get away from John fast enough to avoid questions such as "How do you respond to the rumors that you're evil?" and "Do you think Richie Sambora [her Bon Jovi boyfriend] will be the next mayor of Palm Springs?" This last question, which indirectly poked fun at Sonny Bono, was asked as Cher was slamming her limo door and speeding off. John broke into a full sprint in an attempt to chase down Arsenio Hall. He finally did catch up with the butt of many of Howard's jokes, only to have Arsenio blow him off.

Whereas Sam Donaldson can pull off a quality interview with a politician but has a hard time interviewing a showbiz star, and Barbara Walters is more at ease with the actors of the world than with the politicians, John shows that he has the versatility that a lot of good interviewers lack. He can conduct great interviews with politicians as well as he does with actors and actresses. Actually, John is probably the only interviewer who is tougher than Sam Donaldson on Washington's elite. For example, he asked Walter Mondale, "Did you ever worry that Ferraro would get cramps in office?"

Of course, not everyone is as happy with John's success as I am. There are certain fellow broadcasters who are obviously a bit jealous of Mr. Melendez. It makes me sick to think that there is such petty jealousy in the industry, especially against someone who has managed to overcome the potentially debilitating handicap of a speech impediment in a vocation that relies on speech.

Here is an example of what I am talking about. At a fundraiser for the rain forest, John got a chance to interview one of his forefathers in the industry, Walter Cronkite. He asked Walter, "Are you here because you care about the rain forest or because your publicist thought it was a good idea?" Walter, obviously worried that John was on the verge of showing America that maybe he is not as trustworthy as we have all thought, began to berate the young interviewer. "Oh, come on. That's a ridiculous question. . . . That's a dumb question. Dumb, dumb, dumb." John, being the professional that he is, did not get into a pissing contest with Walter, but instead forged on. "After smoking pot and cheating on his wife, who does Bill Clinton—" he began to ask. Walter must have sensed that John was going for the kill, and stomped off right in the middle of the question.

Mr. Cronkite is not the only fellow broadcaster who seems to be put off by this young, rising star. When John asked *60 Minutes* veteran Mike Wallace, "How can you be so old and still have pimples?" Mike responded by not only insulting John, but also by using a blatant interview ploy—he answered a question with a question: ". . . How can *you* be so young and look the way that you do?" Mike, who has made a career out of asking tough questions and putting people on the spot, would not allow John to ask him another question, and walked away.

Dan Rather was a bit more gracious than his predecessor at CBS News. He did, however, seem very nervous around the young stutterer. John, probably going out of his way to show Mr. Rather that he is not afraid of the tough question, started out by asking, "What's the frequency, Kenneth?" This was the question that a mugger had asked Dan Rather in New York's Central Park immediately before beating him up. Dan responded to this by laughing uncomfortably.

Already, John seemed to have Mr. Rather on the ropes. When John asked him about Howard Stern, Dan stated that he did not know him. This left John in a state of amazement, and he noted that Howard is "like the King of New York." He continued, "You don't know him? Oh my God." After John berated Dan for not knowing who Howard Stern is, they had a classic exchange that played out like some type of Abbott and Costello bit.

John: Who's your favorite Judd?

Dan: Judge?

John: Yeah, Judd.

Dan: Favorite judge. Hmmm.

John: No, no. Judd, Judd.

Dan: Favorite jug. I don't know; usually I drink Wild Turkey or something. I don't know.

Can you imagine what the top brass at CBS must have thought when they saw their number one anchorman involved in the above conversation with a stuttering interviewer? To put a fitting conclusion on a classic piece of television reporting, John ended with, "Do you check after you're done wiping?" It was at this point that someone whisked Mr. Rather away, but not before he stated, "That's all right; we can have a sense of humor about it." I can't help but believe that it was this interview that led to the hiring of Connie Chung to help relieve some of the burden from Dan Rather's shoulders. You see, Connie has had her own run-in with the famed Stutterer; but she handled herself a bit more professionally than Mr. Rather.

Stuttering John asked both Connie Chung and husband Maury Povich, "Whose fault is it that you can't get pregnant?" Maury laughed hysterically, demonstrating why he was the one hosting *A Current Affair*, and answered, "Howard's." Connie was much more reserved and answered, "Yours," referring to John. They quickly scooted away before John could get off another question. The top brass at CBS may have considered Connie to have shown very good judgment as opposed to Dan Rather, who was too confused to even comprehend the question and instead talked about Wild Turkey.

Out of the top interviewers and broadcasters today, Barbara Walters was probably the least intimidated by John. When John asked her if it "pissed her off" that she could not get Howard Stern to do her interview show, she replied, "It makes me very upset. Been trying for years. He's the one we want the most." She did get a bit flustered when John asked her, "Do you think other people who talk like Elmer Fudd should pursue a

IS JOHN BEING EXPLOITED?

The September 1991 issue of *Rolling Stone* magazine featured an article on Stuttering John. In it, Ira Zimmerman, who represents a group called the "National Stuttering Project," asserted that Howard Stern was not only exploiting John, but that he was also "giving people the impression that it's okay to make fun of someone who stutters." Howard's reply to Mr. Zimmerman was "I disagree that we make fun of John because he stutters. We make fun of John because he's wacky." Hey, Howard doesn't make any more fun of John's stutter than he does of Gary's teeth, Jackie's belly, or Robin's breasts. Besides, how many other employers would give a stutterer a job as a celebrity interviewer?

Stuttering John with Sebastian Bach and Snake Sabo of Skid Row. (Lydia Criss/Star File)

future in journalism?" But she came out of it like a trooper when John finished with "Do you have any suggestions on how I can be a better interviewer?" Her tongue-in-cheek response showed quite a good sense of humor and earned her my instant respect. "I think you have to be a little more aggressive. You're too shy," she told John.

John has been able to carve out quite a little reputation for himself as being willing to ask the famous folks of this world questions that no one else on TV or radio would have the balls to ask. On top of that, John has been able to make people more aware that stutterers do exist and that they are normal human beings who can achieve some pretty amazing things, such as asking Oliver North, "Did you ever have a nightmare where your penis gets caught in a paper shredder?" Or asking the Dalai Lama, "Do people ever say 'Hello, Dalai'?" (To which Richard Gere—a follower of the Dalai Lama—interjected, "These are very odd questions.")

John's stutter may be his trademark, but it's his intestinal fortitude that has made him "Hero of the Stupid," as well as a hero to all Stern fans.

CHAPTER 10

THE UNDERPANTS AND NEGLIGEE PARTY

Howard's first attempt to show the world that he could be successful on television was the "Howard Stern's Underpants and Negligee Party." This pay-per-view special was a live version of the radio show, with one difference: The members of the audience were clad only in their underwear. In fact, you could not get into the studio unless you were outfitted in some type of undergarment.

This was not Howard's best work, but you must remember that it was his first-ever television effort. I can remember seeing it live, and the real beauty behind this event was that it was the first time a lot of us got to see what Howard, Robin, Jackie, and Fred looked like. This alone was worth the price of the show. It was also the first time I realized that Robin is an African American. And although I say this was not Howard's best work on television or video, that is only in comparison to what he has done since. When the show aired in 1988, this was something completely new, innovative, and daring, and extremely entertaining. Since then, Howard Stern has kept getting better.

However, if you have not yet seen "Howard Stern's Underpants and Negligee Party," and you get the opportunity to see it, you'll be witnessing the beginnings of a great television career. You will also see a lot of the regular guests who still appear on his show. Featured on the show are Richard Belzer, Penn & Teller, Emo Phillips, Judy Tenuta, Steve Rossi of the comedy team Allen and Rossi, and , of course, Jessica Hahn. Also appearing is "Bloated Attorney" Dominic Barbara, who most recently represented Joey Buttaffuoco during his statutory rape case (and you'll be surprised at just how big he is). You will also get to see "Siobhan."

Siobhan is, or at least was, a man who wanted to undergo a sex change operation but could not afford it. It turned out the only reason Siobhan was invited to the show was because some guy in the audience had agreed to "tongue-kiss" him. The guy who agreed to this tried to back out, but after being threatened with removal from the show by Howard, he kissed Siobhan. Siobhan, who at the time was awaiting the results of his AIDS test, quickly protested after the kiss, "No tongue!"

Robin, finally came out to help get things rolling with the TV version of "Lesbian Dial-a-Date." Howard, who was at this point in only his black underwear (with suspenders), finally got to the phone calls while the beautiful Alexis, one of the lesbian participants, deep-throated a banana covered in whipped cream. By the time they got a woman caller on the phone, they had run out of time.

Howard later introduced Leslie West, who used to appear a lot more regularly on the radio show than he does now. Leslie was a member of the legendary rock group Mountain, and he did a solo version of the band's famous hit "Mississippi Queen." It was not very good, but it was fun to see what Leslie West looked like compared with his earlier days. Let's just say he is a "mountain" of a man.

Yes, and we finally met "Becky, the Mental Patient." Until this show she had gone by the name of Denise, but at this point she decided to start going by the name of Becky, which was one of her multiple personalities. Becky revealed that she got a leave from her mental hospital just so she could be on the show. Of course, Howard was flattered, and he offered her this compliment: "For a mental case, your breasts aren't that bad."

The highlight of the show had to be the guy who lit his penis on fire. The guy, who claimed to be Joe Franklin's producer, actually stripped down to his underwear, had Robin squirt a healthy amount of lighter fluid directly on his crotch, then proceeded to try to fry an egg in a pan while his crotch went up in flames.

Leslie West in his younger days. This photo is vintage 1977. (Chuck Pulin/Star File)

ANOTHER PAY-PER-VIEW EVENT TO REMEMBER

Howard Stern's second pay-per-view special took place on New Year's Eve, 1994. The event billed as the "Miss Howard Stern New Year's Eve Pageant" was the most successful project in pay-per-view history. The show was watched by more than 375,000 households, and each was billed $39.95. Many newspapers reported that Howard raked in as much as $12 million from the three-hour spectacular; ultimately, the show grossed between $15 and $16 million.

If you were one of the few Stern fans that did not get a chance to see the show, don't panic, Howard has released the show on videotape and it can be ordered by dialing 800–52–Stern. He is forcing all of his really fanatical fans who watched (and taped) on New Year's Eve to also purchase the video because it includes never-before seen backstage footage shot at the party after the show.

The live "beauty pageant" which took place in Newark, New Jersey, featured celebrity judges such as boxing's Joe Frazier, Sherman Hemsley of "The Jeffersons," Mark Hamil, of *Star Wars* fame, and even John Wayne Bobbitt. Howard held a telethon for John during the broadcast which featured a re-enactment of the night John had his penis severed by his wife, Lorena. Although Howard offered John Wayne Bobbitt $15,000 to show the world his penis, John turned it down. Heck, there was no reason for John to drop his pants at that point, as Howard had already raised close to $200,000 for John through the phone calls which were pouring in to the show

to offer
money to help defer
medical costs and to get a "free"
commemorative penis-slicing T-shirt,
featuring a picture of a knife-wielding
woman on one side and reading "Love Hurts"
on the other. Other memorable moments from
the show included the opening skit in which
Howard portrayed Michael Jackson torturing
a young boy, Howard and Sherman Hemsley as Ted
Danson (in black face) and Whoopie Goldberg, and
Howards appearance on stage of the beauty pageant seated on a toilet bowl with his pants down around his ankles.
The beauty pageant itself (if you could call it that) featured
a wide range of both talent and beauty. Many of the girls were
topless but some of them really shouldn't have been. One contestant, in a particularly distasteful display, dumped a very
large jar full of maggots into her mouth as part of the talent
portion of the show while another sang a song about anal sex.
Overall, the show was a shock-a-minute affair with some really hilarious bits and one-liners thrown in. Of course Howard
can't do anything without pissing someone off.
This time, Stern angered the government officials of Newark
when he called the town the "carjacking capital of the world"
and a "piece of shit city" during the live telecast. One Newark councilman stated that Newark had "been disgraced,
embarrassed across the nation." The same councilman
than went on to help sell Howard's beauty pageant
video with the backstage footage by stating that a
"lewd and immoral" party followed the show. "The
sex that took place . . . was worse than any porn
show," was the comment made to the press
by the councilman. Howard should send
this man a thank-you note and few old
copies of "Butt-Bongo Fiesta"
that he might have
lying around.

Howard got off his best line of the show right before the guy lit up: "I love the smell of burning penis in the morning." Anyway, the guy lit his crotch and began cooking the egg. Soon it was obvious that the fire was getting too hot for him, and he ended up having to rip his underwear off. He stood there completely naked, but instead of covering himself up, he then sprayed lighter fluid on his bare buttocks and proceeded to light his ass on fire. He quickly patted that out, but was rewarded anyway with the loudest cheers of the night. Now that was something to tell the grandchildren about.

Later on in the show we were entertained by a classic bit of tape entitled "Bum Makeover." In this episode, Howard sent out "Mitch the Intern" (who was later replaced on the Stern team by Stuttering John) to find a homeless person on whom to perform a more complete makeover than the beauty makeovers you see on the *Oprah Winfrey Show*. They found a homeless person by the name of Anthony Bartow who was living down in the subway in New York City. First, Mitch offered him a haircut, shave, and new suit, and promised to send him on a shopping spree. He agreed, and they put him in a limo and took him to a hotel for a shower and shave.

As soon as the shopping spree ended, Anthony was put in the limousine again and driven directly back to the subway stop where he had been found. Mitch presented him with free gifts, including luggage from E Vincent, a bonsai plant, Butter Buds, cigarettes, and, of course, a mattress from Dial-A-Mattress. The camera then panned back to show Anthony sitting all by himself in a subway station with all of his sandwiches and soda from the shopping spree, as well as his bonsai plant and new mattress. They left him exactly where they'd found him.

At one point in the video, Howard brings out Fred Norris as Kurt Waldheim Jr. He stated, "I am a simple fry cook from Austria" and added that "baby penis" tastes a lot like chicken. After turning his attention to "Scott the Engineer," he stated, "I have found a cure for your baldness. It is called bull semen."

The hard part is to have a two-thousand-pound steer stand over your head while you jerk him off." Kurt's version of minoxidil gave way to a game of "Guess Who's the Jew."

"Howard Stern's Underpants and Negligee Party" was the first of four videotapes that Howard has sold through his 800-52-STERN telephone sales number. If you don't have this video, you are missing out on Howard's first successful foray into the world of television. All of Howard's videos are on sale for a limited amount of time and then automatically become collector's items. This being Howard's first such project, it will be the video hardest to come by and probably will end up the most collectible.

If you can track down an old copy of this classic, consider yourself lucky and pay the price to have it forever. It is well worth it just to see the guy light his penis on fire, but throw in the "Bum Makeover" and Kurt Waldheim Jr. and you definitely get your money's worth. Like I said, it is not as good as his two later videos, but it is still very funny and is your only chance to see some of the regulars like Becky and Siobhan as well as Steve Rossi and Leslie West. Okay, now, everyone put your clothes back on.

11 CHAPTER

U.S. OPEN SORES

f anyone thought that Howard Stern listeners were people who were just interested in the shock value of the show but were not real fans of Howard and his brand of comedy, the "U.S. Open Sores" event would prove them seriously wrong. In 1989, Howard Stern sold out the Nassau Coliseum on Long Island; the arena holds 16,000 people, and he did it in *four hours*! Not only that, but he sold it out for an event billed as a tennis "grudge" match between him and his producer, Boy Gary, who are two of the least athletic people you will ever see. No other disc jockey in the world would have been able to inspire fans to shell out $22.50 for such an event, and very few celebrities—right down to the hottest rock groups—would have been able to sell out an arena of that size in four hours. Promoter Ron Delsener, who promotes big-name rock concerts, called the four-hour sellout "extraordinary."

The event at the Coliseum was turned into "Howard Stern's U.S. Open Sores," his second videotape sold over his 800-52-STERN telephone sales line. My own personal evaluation of the tape is that it is much better than "Underpants" but not nearly as good as Howard's next video, "Butt Bongo Fiesta." It is still a very entertaining tape, however, and you should try and find a copy of it. We all need to urge Howard to rerelease all of his videos as his audience continues to expand.

Howard Stern also knows how to give his fans exactly what they want. The "U.S. Open Sores" video not only takes us backstage at the end of the event, but we get to see a lot of the activities leading up to the actual show. We also get our first-ever look into the radio studio where Howard works every weekday.

The tape shows him interviewing and giving advice to the ball girls for the tennis match. The advice consists of telling one girl that she needs to pull her panties farther into the crack of her ass, like the rest of the girls. When she turns around to show Howard her ass and still has not gotten the hang of it, one of the other ball girls—showing the kind of teamwork a ball girl can be proud of—helps by reaching out and giving the slower girl the kind of "wedgie" that Howard is looking for. After Gary helps put a pasty on a breast of one of the girls (Gary, I don't ever want to hear you complain about your job again), Howard says, "Well, boys, you got that all on video? Get that to me quick."

Howard is the only person who could take an argument on the radio over who is the better athlete, he or Boy Gary, and turn it into a major event at the Nassau Coliseum.

When Howard emerged from the tunnel at the Coliseum and made his way up to the stage, you would have thought

Elvis had just entered the building. The fans went crazy and the place came alive, and began a buzz in the stands that continued throughout the event.

Howard and Robin first introduced "Celestine," a black woman without arms and legs who plays the keyboard with her tongue. Celestine proceeded to play an amazing version of "The Star-Spangled Banner," to a rousing ovation from the crowd.

The first major event of the evening was the tennis match between Robin and "Darren the Foot Licker." Darren is a geek who used to write to Robin daily to tell her how much in love with her he was and how he wanted to suck on her toes and lick her feet. He is the type of person most celebrities would report to the police immediately. However, being the good friend that he is, Howard decided to call the guy instead. He turned Darren into a regular guest, even having him in to suck on Robin's feet one day.

After telling Darren on many occasions that there was no way she would ever be interested in him, Robin agreed to this tennis match as a way to bring the episode to a close, one way or the other. The bet was that if Robin beat Darren, he would have to stop all contact with her; if Darren was victorious, Robin would have to go out on a date with him. You could feel the tension in the stadium.

There to call the score for the big match was that famous guest stutterer, "Quentin the Stutterer" [a poor slob whose speech impediment was ten times worse than Stuttering John's]. Also participating were the ball boys, consisting of a one-legged guy and a guy in a wheelchair. (Howard was really showing his appreciation of the handicapped community that night.) A fired-up Robin battled back to take the second game after losing the first, to set up the thrilling tiebreaker. With victory only points away, Darren, it was obvious, could almost taste Robin's feet. Unfortunately for the ponytailed toe taster, the crowd turned viciously against him and began a chant of "Darren Sucks"—and I don't believe they were referring to feet.

Robin jumped out to a lead in the third and final game, and it looked like Darren's dream of sucking foot (at least Robin's) was coming to an end when all of a sudden she missed an easy volley. In his own unique way, "Kurt Waldheim" let the crowd know that it isn't over until it's over: "Don't put away the K-Y yet." It was only a matter of seconds, though, before Robin took the final point and ended the foot licker's dream of ever tonguing her chocolaty toe treats. Robin, a thrilled victor, told the foot licker that he could never again bother her or lick her feet, but I believe Darren broke his promise, and Robin later began receiving letters once again from her foot lover.

The next match was the feature event of the evening and pitted the flabby Boy Gary Dell'Abate against the tall, uncoordinated Radio God, Howard Stern. With "Grampa" Al Lewis and Robin doing the commentating and "Elephant Boy" brought in specially to do the score, we were set up for quite an exciting best-of-seven tennis showdown. However, the match went all Gary's way. Although Howard blamed the loss on a scoring error by "Elephant Boy," it was obvious that "Cum Gums" was the better player.

Howard, who lost the match four games to two, compounded his loss with one of the worst displays of poor sportsmanship ever recorded; he would have made John McEnroe very, very proud. "You suck my ass, you pimple-faced, douche foam bag," Howard yelled at his horse-teethed boy producer.

We also again saw Vinnie Mazzeo, the guy who lit his penis on fire during the "Underpants and Negligee Party." This time he sprayed lighter fluid on the baseball cap he was wearing and set it on fire. He then stood there and tried to tell a joke that no one understood. When he finally took the hat off, his hair was on fire and he had to pat it out by hand. He was smiling the entire time.

After putting the flame out on the top of his head, he began dousing himself with lighter fluid all over his body. This really started to worry the crew, and they tried to dump some water on him. Robin was obviously worried that a human life was about to be lost, and she implored, "You've got to get away from the tennis courts." Vinnie ended up lighting himself and standing on his head. After he had briefly served as a human torch, the crew quickly put the flames out with buckets of water.

Vinnie was extremely pissed at Howard's crew for doing this, so Howard called him up to the microphones and told him there had been smoke "coming out of his head." Vinnie replied, "I know there was. I know there was. I have no fucking hair as it is, so I don't care." (I believe that the word "brains" could easily be substituted for the word "hair" in the sentence above.)

Howard brought on one hot performer after another. The next guest was former *Penthouse* pet Kimberly Taylor. Kimberly was brought out to be hypnotized by Dr. Marshall King, the resident guest hypnotist. Before they got started, Howard complimented her on her *Penthouse* layout, telling her he'd especially enjoyed the "lesbian shots." Kimberly was offended by this and claimed there were no lesbian pictures. Howard countered, "You were sitting there eating out some girl's cunt and you're going to tell me these aren't lesbian pictures?" Excellent point on Howard's part, and I think any photographer skilled in this area would agree that, yes, they qualify as lesbian shots.

The major problem with this whole bit was that, in my opinion, Kimberly was never really hypnotized, and was not even very good at faking it. At one point, when Dr. King went to put her back into her deep sleep, she muttered "Sorry," instead of just going to sleep like all of Dr. King's other subjects. She also started bobbing her head around when she believed Dr. King was about to bring her out of the deep sleep, before he actually did. Even Howard admitted, while talking to Robin at the end of this tape, that he had his doubts.

Don't get me wrong: I do believe that Dr. King is very capable of hypnotizing people. On one of Howard's TV shows, he demonstrated this by having a hypnotized male subject feel up Boy Gary and getting him to believe that Gary was a beautiful girl. If you saw that show, you know that the guy acted nothing like Kimberly did. I think it's time Kimberly went back on

Sam Kinison on stage with Malika and Sabrina. (Chuck Pulin/Star File)

Howard's radio show and made a public confession and apology, not so much for faking that she was hypnotized, but for her poor acting. Her appearance was the only time that I have ever felt cheated by a Howard Stern bit.

We got to see "Gina (as in "va-gina") Man" and "Crazy Jerry," who were also regulars on the radio show. Gina Man is a mentally disturbed person who loved to tell jokes; unfortunately, I think he must make them up himself. He told several dandies to the Coliseum crowd. "This is Mother Teresa speaking from the bed. God don't want me yet, man. I've got more feet to taste." This really cracked up both him and Crazy Jerry, who looks like he belongs in a Cheech and Chong movie and seems to serve as Gina Man's handler. Unfortunately for all of us, the first joke was the most tasteful of the evening, and the only one that made any sense at all.

The highlight of the evening was round two between Jessica and Sam. Howard wanted to take this opportunity to try and bring Sam and Jessica back together, much as he and Sam had been brought back together after having it out on the radio show. Jessica was first to enter, dressed in a low-cut black Frederick's of Hollywood type outfit and looking gorgeous. Sam entered the arena with Malika and her sister Sabrina.

Immediately, the fireworks started, as Jessica expressed her anger that Sam had not had "the balls" to come out alone.

Soon, Jessica and Malika were stinging each other with verbal assaults. Malika told the audience that Jessica is "working her way through the alphabet" when it comes to men. Jessica countered by claiming that Malika had breast surgery because she wanted her breasts to be as pert as Jessica's. A naked mud wrestling match certainly could have settled this little cat fight rather nicely.

After an extended war of words between Sam and Jessica, Howard seemed to give up on his quest to bring the former lovers back together. The audience, however, seemed to physically be saying to Howard, "Don't give up yet. You can do it. You're the King of Radio, for Christ's sake."

Howard couldn't understand why Jessica was being so stubborn in her refusal to make peace. "All he did was fall asleep," he told her. Howard didn't realize that all he was doing was making things worse, as Malika jumped in with "Shows you how good she is." Jessica rebounded with a very nice counterpunch: "No, honey, that was because you weren't able to please him." Malika then took another shot at her female foe, saying, "You never had one on one, Jessica." Again, Jessica is up for the challenge: "Oh yeah, Malika, and you should know. What are you doing with that other girl and your sister and Sam?" (At least we know Sam had one fucking great life before he was taken from us.)

Well, the two ex-lovebirds finally put their differences aside long enough for Jessica to appear onstage with Sam during his spectacular rendition of "Wild Thing." The capacity crowd went wild as Leslie West and Pig Vomit began to play Sam's hit song, and rushed the stage as Sam began to sing.

Malika and Sabrina, in hot outfits, wiggled their asses for the crowd on one side of the stage while Jessica danced on the other. Partway into the song, Jessica reached out to Sam and they sang a line or two, before Malika rushed over and pushed her out of the way. As security guards worked hard to keep the crowd from swamping the stage, Howard took off with a wave. Sam sang a couple of lines with Robin before the song ended, at which point he and his girls rushed off the stage in order to escape the out-of-control crowd.

Backstage, we got to see Howard's sister Ellen, as well as our first-ever glimpse at his mother and father, looking and acting like the typical proud parents.

We also saw Vinnie D'Amico, the guy who would later eat a plate of live earthworms on Howard's TV show. On this night, he limited himself to banging a steel pot on his head, then lying on a bed of nails while someone used a sledgehammer to break a slab of concrete that had been placed on his chest. (Do you think this Vinnie is any relation to the Vinnie who lights his penis and other parts of his body on fire?)

I love the backstage portions of Howard's videos, as we get to meet the people that we hear from on the radio a lot, such as the late, great "Ted the Janitor." He was hanging backstage after the show and told Howard when asked what he would do if he were alone with Robin: "Oh, Robin. I would just grab the boobies . . . kiss the boobies and play with the hairy patch. Try to get the snatch." Ted always had a way with words. He must have been a great date.

Also, in a very touching moment, the video recorded Gina Man getting a "Bronsky" from "Rachel the Spanker," in memory of the late "Froggie." ("Froggie" was a regular caller on the show back when I first started listening; his nickname was fitting, as he sounded like a frog.) For those of you who do not know breast slang, a Bronsky is when a girl allows you to put your face between her breasts and then sort of smothers you with them. Thus, if you ever hear of anyone who suffered "death by Bronsky," you can always count on the stiff having a smile on his face at the wake.

Finally, as the credits rolled, there was Howard, oil-wrestling with a few nearly naked babes. Good ending, good video.

CHAPTER 12

"BUTT BONGO FIESTA"

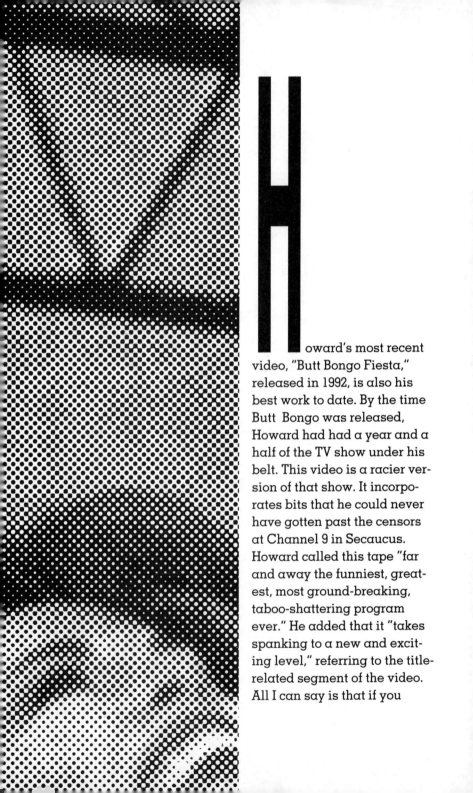

Howard's most recent video, "Butt Bongo Fiesta," released in 1992, is also his best work to date. By the time Butt Bongo was released, Howard had had a year and a half of the TV show under his belt. This video is a racier version of that show. It incorporates bits that he could never have gotten past the censors at Channel 9 in Secaucus. Howard called this tape "far and away the funniest, greatest, most ground-breaking, taboo-shattering program ever." He added that it "takes spanking to a new and exciting level," referring to the title-related segment of the video. All I can say is that if you loved the TV show and/or his two previous videos, this is a can't-miss for you.

This is the only video in which Howard played "Jungleman," conquering "big, sloppy, naked, titty women in 3-D." Also on the tape is the actual date between Capital Janks and the Philadelphia Zoo Keeper's wife. Another highlight of the tape has got to be the "Guess Who's the Jew" segment with the KKK Guy.

Howard, clad in his early '70s Mad Hasidic Jew outfit, and doing his best Jim Lange (of the old *Dating Game*) impression, was at his game show best. He introduced "Kurt Waldheim Jr." (Fred Norris) first, then brought out everyone's favorite racist, the KKK Guy, Daniel Carver. Daniel, in full KKK garb, took off his hood and was welcomed by Howard to "Guess Who's the Jew." Sitting next to the KKK Guy was Marie Bronson, an African-American woman who—surprise!—did not seem to subscribe to Mr. Carver's views. (It's amazing, but for some reason, every time Howard puts a member of the Ku Klux Klan in the same room with an African American, things seem to get hostile.) Howard, with his keen sense of perception, could sense hostility in the room, and tried to defuse it by reminding the two adversaries that it was only a game show.

In order to make everyone happy, Howard allowed the KKK Guy to display his KKK T-shirts, which proclaimed the following messages of goodwill: "Warning—nine of ten niggers are polluted by AIDS" and "The Original Boys in the Hood," featuring a picture of Klansmen standing in full regalia in front of the American flag. The best part of the segment came when they rolled out a board with a list of derogatory slang terms for various ethnic groups and asked the KKK Guy to put them in the order in which they belong on the KKK evolutionary scale. The KKK Guy told Howard that "the Jew is the lowest" and, without even trying to be funny, uttered this gem: "And I'd put a gay right under him . . . right on top of him, I guess." Next Howard questioned Daniel's judgment in saying that the black man is higher on the evolutionary scale than gays. The KKK Guy

responded, "Well, [blacks] are animals, but according to the Bible the gays should be put to death. Niggers just should be with their own animals." (Jeez, Howard, what are you, stupid, you moron?)

After the KKK Guy finally had the order straight, Howard stated, "Well, I tell you, it's very, very confusing, this whole pecking order." I think everyone would agree with this observation.

After the game show ended, Howard decided to delve a little deeper into the psyche of the KKK Guy, and it is quite revealing. Howard asked him what types of shows he watched on television. Mr. Carver answered "cartoons," which led Howard to say, "Serious guy like yourself. What cartoons do you like?" The KKK Guy replied that he liked "all of them." Pushing on, Howard then asked our hooded animation lover, "Who is your favorite cartoon character?" Remaining noncommitted, the KKK Guy replied, "I don't know," (However, I think we can pretty much rule out anyone in the old "Fat Albert and Friends" cartoon.)

Also on this video is probably one of the most important tributes you'll ever have a chance to witness, Howard Stern's "Tribute to the Vagina." For this segment, Howard dressed in a tuxedo, and why not—it was a big event. Soon we saw Robin, dressed in a beautiful black gown but for some reason seated on a bidet. (When Howard asked her why she had her dress on, Robin answered, "Because my vagina's not dirty." Jeez, Robin, thanks for sharing that with us.)

After a brief history lesson about the vagina, they soon came upon a woman who happened to be lying around the studio with her legs up in stirrups. We got to see her breasts, which is always fun, but apparently Robin and Howard did not think that was intimate enough, so they shrank themselves down and entered her vagina. They put on raincoats and Howard decided to wear a clothespin on his nose as he said, "What a smell, Robin. Don't you want one of these clothespins I'm wearing?" Robin replied, "No, Howard, it's a familiar smell to me." (Now either Robin was telling us something about her sexual preference or she should have received some Summer's Eve feminine hygiene products for Christmas.)

Before Howard and Robin could exit the vagina, a wire clothes hanger entered the picture. When Robin raised the spectre of a possible illegal abortion, Howard stated, "Either that or she sat on her dry cleaning."

The next part of the tribute found Stuttering John on the street asking the common man and woman their thoughts regarding the vagina. A fascinating conversation took place between John and one female participant. John, being the shy guy he is, asked, "Do you have a nickname for your vagina?" The equally shy female responded, "No, but my breasts are Fred and Ethel." Hmm, I wonder if she would like to meet my little Ricky.

The best portion of the tribute had Jessica Hahn coming onstage in a totally see-through body stocking. She looked absolutely fabulous and was hiding nothing. Jessica definitely gave the audience the feeling that she was proud of her vagina and thought it deserving of a tribute. This was also probably the funniest interview that Howard has ever done, which is saying a hell of a lot.

Howard did a really in-depth (pun intended) interview with Ms. Hahn about her "fuzzy lap flounder." First we learned that Jessica sprouted her first curly locks on her "bearded clam" when she was twelve or thirteen. Unbelievably, Howard then asked, "How many fingers is uncomfortable?" and had the nerve to claim, "That's a legitimate question." Jessica obviously disagreed, as she refused to answer. Howard, not discouraged at all, kept plugging away. "Did a guy ever miss your vagina and go in the wrong place?" After much coercion, Jessica eventually admitted, "It could happen." That was as good as a confession to Howard.

I'm not sure how Howard manages to come up with all the original ideas for game shows, but "Pick Your Partner's Vagina" had to be one of the best. I only wish he could have gotten Vanna White to somehow participate in the game. The unique premise behind this game show was to blindfold a male and have him try to guess which of the female participants was his girlfriend by the smell of their fingers, the smell being obtained by inserting two fingers into their respective vaginas. According to Howard, the object of the game was for the male guest to figure out "which one of our 'cuntestants' is his spouse."

To the sheer amazement of the male guest, he picked the wrong female. I'm still wondering if it's possible that somehow his spouse's fingers ended up in the wrong vagina. The other possible reason for the guest having messed up his selection is that his spouse put her finger up the wrong hole. He did have a horrible grimace on his face while one of the girls held her fingers under his nose. Hey, shit happens; just ask Jessica.

One bit of interesting information which Howard shared with us during the tribute was: "According to studies, only forty percent of men find the vagina fragrance sexually arousing. Yet ninety percent of the same men love to smell their own farts." Kotex ought to keep this in mind when developing the next scent for its deodorant maxipads.

There you have it, Howard Stern's touching tribute to the vagina. I think it would be only fair to see a tribute to the penis courtesy of Oprah Winfrey or Sally Jessy Raphael in the near future.

Another highlight on this video was a combination of perhaps Howard's two favorite themes, game shows and lesbians, with a reprise of "Lesbian Love Connection." Our first lesbian was introduced by Robin as "Leeza, a coffee exporter from Colombia [who] loves wild lesbian sex." (Man, I wish they'd focused more on that coffee exporting stuff.) Leeza is extremely cute and had already chosen "Claire" on some previous show to be her date. This was the follow-up show, with video footage from that date.

They went to a restaurant, where Leeza declared, "I love fish." (Why is that funny? Please refer back to the "Tribute to the Vagina" segment. Thank you) Claire decided that over dinner at a fancy restaurant was the best time to explain to us her preference for lesbian sex. "With a man, you know if you give him what he wants right away, ciao, he's gone. You'll never hear from him again, 'cause once he fucks you that's the end, right? But with a woman it's a different story, because if they like it and they enjoy you then they're going to want more and keep coming back." I don't feel qualified to comment too much on Claire's opinions about lesbians, but it sure sounds like there were a few guys who used to get very lucky with Claire before she discovered muff diving.

Next Leeza told us about her first lesbian experience, which was so hot that Bob Woolybush was overheard saying, "Whoa, whoa, whoa, a 2.5 on the boner meter." That was a pretty high reading for Bob, who did not look to be the most masculine of game show hosts. And the meter probably jumped up another notch when Leeza began imitating the sound of multiple orgasms.

After some dancing, the two luscious lesbians ended up back at their hotel room. There, not only did Leeza expose her lovely, luscious, lesbian love lumps (for you tongue-twister fans), but she also demonstrated how she would perform oral sex on Claire. Isn't that special? As Claire's head was just about to go for Leeza's breasts, the camera faded out and we went back to the studio, where Bob Woolybush stated, "I bet you're both good at licking stamps."

On this superb video, you also get to see the winners from the "Gross Video Contest" that Howard ran. These clips were just like those you would see on *America's Funniest Home Videos*, if the show originated from hell. One video had an Easter theme to it, and I wouldn't be surprised if it showed up in a few Easter baskets this year. It showed the cutest little furry bunny humping a red balloon.

Another video would only be appreciated by those of you who enjoyed seeing Gary eat shit in the Jungleman skit. This one had a guy picking his nose with his tongue. For those keep-

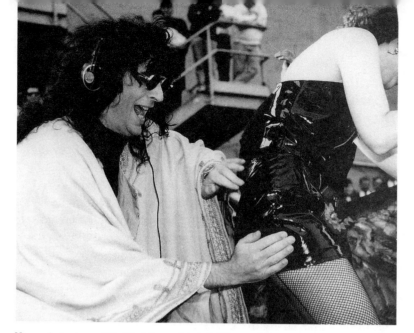

Howard playing a little "Butt Bongo" in L.A. (Vincent Zuffante/Star File)

ing score at home, yes, he struck pay dirt and, yes, he swallowed. Uuughh!!!

One of the last videos had a guy blow himself out of bed and out a window when he farted. Not real funny. No way this deserved to be discussed in the same breath as the balloon-humping bunny.

At the end of this tape is the title cut from the video, "Howard Estern's Butt Bongo." To my knowledge, this is the first-ever game show devoted *entirely* to the playing of music on the backsides of women. "Butt Bongo" was first featured on the radio show, as Howard had contestants come down and compete for Bruce Springsteen tickets. The video version of "Butt Bongo" moves away from the pounding beat of rock 'n' roll in favor of a more traditional Latin sound.

Our host, "Howardo," introduced the first couple, beautiful blond Stacy and Eric, and asked Stacy in a very bad Spanish costume and even worse accent, "You got blond crotcho too?" Stacy, another shy girl, began to pull aside her G-string to prove that she did in fact have a blond crotcho, but was stopped abruptly from doing so—however, not before Howardo got to view "uno pequito hairs." Howardo, apparently not having gotten enough of a thrill from Stacy's pubic peep show, next asked her to bend over with her ass facing the camera. As she was doing this favor for the audience, he stated, "I see mucho hemorrhoidos," which really sort of ruined the moment.

Next, Stacy was told to lie across Eric's legs, where he began using her derriere like a set of bongo drums. Eric was encouraged to play her behind as loudly as he could, since this was what the judges were looking for in deciding who would win the "Butt Bongo" game. Eric did suspiciously well, leading one to believe that he was not an amateur at this sport, and leaving Stacy's buttocks a lovely shade of crimson.

Jerome and Sue were the next couple, with Jerome going wild on Sue's butt. Although Jerome played loudly, I think the judges probably gave him lower scores than Eric in the style category.

Up next was an interracial lesbian threesome in which a black man beat the asses of two large, homely lesbian ladies as they knelt before him and tongue-kissed. (It was good to finally see a sport where men and women of all colors and creeds can participate with a equal chance at victory.)

The two big lesbians were not going to get past Howardo without his getting in a little dig about their size. "I'll tell you about these lesbians: If they had a penis once in a while, it would knock some weight off them," the host deadpanned while the girls' butts were being bounced around by the guy. I have to admit, both girls' cheeks were very red; however, this guy had a lot more butt to work with than Eric or Jerome had. The judges went with Stacy and Eric. It was hard to disagree with them but sometimes it's just a shame there can only be one winner.

The end of the video consists of a behind-the-scenes look into the making of the video, Howard Stern style. These intimate moments include the makeup guy putting the long green boogers into Gary's nose for the Jungleman skit; the elephant in Jungleman taking multiple dumps; and breasts, breasts, breasts. A girl who did a dog imitation earlier in the video adds a new and exciting twist to her act: She has the dog squeal like it's been hit by a car. (It's nice to see someone who does not rest on her laurels and who instead tries to add a new dimension to her talent.) Finally, we get to see a girl who has had her tongue pierced. (Blow job? No thank you.)

If you have not seen "Butt Bongo Fiesta," you have not seen Howard Stern's funniest work ever!!!

13 CHAPTER

THE ADVENTURES OF FARTMAN

There have been many superheroes over the years, with many different powers. Spiderman could spin webs, Aquaman could swim underwater without needing air, The Flash could run at a blinding rate of speed. Superman, of course, not only had superhuman strength, but had X-ray vision and could fly. However, it took Howard Stern to create a superhero with what has got to be the smelliest superpowers this side of Krypton. Yes, it's "Fartman, as brave as he can be" and "passing gas for truth and liberty."

Fartman has been protecting America against her

Fartman showing off his powerful backside at the 1992 MTV Awards. (Vincent Zuffante/Star File)

enemies since at least 1988. That year, Iranians were threatening to take Americans hostage in retaliation for the United States having mistakenly shot down a commercial Iranian airplane which U.S. officials believed to be on a military operation. This is my earliest recollection of Fartman, and I must say I was very impressed with the way he called the Iranian Embassy and demanded that it back off from its calls for terrorism.

The Iranian who picks up the phone at the embassy told Fartman, "When we are talking about the deaths of two hundred and ninety people, it is rather inappropriate to talk about the lives of nine"; but Fartman, bravely and rightly so, told the Iranian that "a human life is a human life" and that the United States had made an "honest" mistake. When Fartman let out a flatulent warning blast of gas, the Iranian mocked him with, "If that makes you feel better." Of course, as any self-respecting superhero knows, you must first try to settle differences with words before you blast your enemies off the face of the earth with noxious ass fumes. Fartman tried to get the Iranian to admit that his country started the hostilities. "You started it," stated Fartman. "Did not," countered the foreign statesman. "Did too," reported the gaseous superhero as he patiently tried to negotiate a peace agreement between the two feuding countries.

Unfortunately, a superhero can never rest for long, as there is always injustice to battle in this cruel world of ours. Fartman came to the aid of Chinese students as they were being crushed by their own government back in 1989. This time, not only did he use his powerful backside odor to threaten the Chinese consulate, but he also backed this up with an effort to start a nationwide boycott of Chinese checkers. Way to go, Fartman!

Fartman comes to the aid of Americans all over the world. After two American nuns were murdered in Nicaragua, the call went out once more for Fartman to rush into action. After placing a call to Nicaragua from his own sort of bat cave (K-Rock's radio studio), Fartman demanded an explanation for the barbaric deed. Realizing that he was not going to get any type of satisfactory answer, he had no alternative but to threaten to "blow a hole in Nicaragua." (Yes, some of you may say that this would have cost a lot of innocent lives. Well, innocent noses, yes, but innocent lives I'm not so sure of.)

"The Prince of Poop," "Baron of Brown Air," and "Master of Methane" is the kind of superhero all America can be proud of. He is there for us whenever America or Americans are threatened by a foreign country or leader. He is as patriotic as Ex-Lax, enemas, and mother's homemade baked beans. Needless to say, Fartman was there for America when she needed him most, during Desert Storm. While the United States stood on the brink of war with a hated Middle East enemy, all noses turned to Fartman, with hopes that he would be able to make this military encounter a quick and painless one for America.

In August of 1990, it happened: Fartman suddenly appeared at the K-rock studios, and the call to the Iraqi

MTV AND FLATULENCE

For those
of you who missed
the MTV Awards appearance
by Fartman, Dana Carvey and Phil
Hartman of *Saturday Night Live* did a
very funny bit while impersonating Johnny
Carson and Ed McMahon, respectively. During
the taped bit, which aired immediately after
Fartman's departure from the awards show,
Johnny asked if Fartman was funny or not. Ed
replied, "Basic rule: Farts equal funny. Yes sir."
Johnny responded, "I did not know that. Is that
what kids like today?" Ed answered, "Yes sir,
they love flatulence." They ended with Johnny
asking Ed to pull his finger. Ed looked
amused and told Johnny, "Know
the joke, sir. Not born
yesterday."

Fartman with Robin and Jessica Hahn at the 1992 MTV Awards. (Vincent Zuffante/Star File)

Embassy went out. Never before had Fartman sounded so pissed and gassy. He told the Iraqis that he would allow them "twenty-four hours" to get their butts out of Kuwait. He also threw at them the threat to end all threats: "We will kill all sheep and your men will have nothing to make love to."

Although Fartman doesn't like to talk about it, I suspect he had something to do with the quick end of Desert Storm. Sure, Stormin' Norman was an imposing fellow, but I'm pretty sure that the malodorous stench emanating from our hero's butt was the final straw in getting that country-stealing, sheep-loving, great-Satan-hating, tail-between-your-legs-running, Bush-bashing, oil-grabbing, nuclear-arsenal-hiding, terrorist-supporting, bunch of sand eaters out of Kuwait. Hey, we're talking about a country known for its use of poison gas; it's only right that the king of all gas, Fartman, should help in bringing it down.

Fartman was a very elusive sort for quite some time. Although we could hear him whenever the United States faced some sort of threat, we never were able to *see* the caped cheese cutter. That was the case, anyway, until he made his first television appearance on *The Howard Stern Show*. "The Adventures of Fartman" sketch included a guest appearance by none other than the original Batman himself, Adam West.

173

Fartman's first-ever TV appearance found him dressed in a brownish caped outfit with a toilet seat draped over his head. He had the trademark ass-cheek cutouts and proceeded to barbecue a chicken with his gaseous emissions.

Fartman made his only other known appearance on the MTV Awards in 1992. Apparently, he has quite the wardrobe, as he appeared in a much fancier, more colorful, caped outfit which included a neon *F* on the front and a huge bulge in the crotch. As a matter of fact, the only resemblance to the original Fartman costume were the cutouts that exposed both ass cheeks. You could tell the nation had not suffered from any serious threats in a while, as Fartman's butt cheeks were awfully flabby.

The sagging ass cheeks of Fartman (aka Howard Stern) even received a "Jeers" from the "Cheers 'n' Jeers" page of *TV Guide*. Ah, screw *TV Guide*, their magazine stinks worse than Fartman's butt. Fartman, who literally flew down from the rafters, was at the awards show to present the "Best Metal Hard-Rock Video" award, along with Luke Perry of *Beverly Hills 90210*. Luke, apparently, was the only star at the show who was willing to introduce the bare-assed gas emitter, and he did so by telling the audience, "It's a bird, it's a plane, it's a really bad smell; ladies and gentlemen, Fartman."

Luke, who was a good sport about the entire event, not only told Fartman that he had a "great ass," but also touched it "for power." After Metallica was announced as the winner of the award for "Enter Sandman," one of the members of the band went over and touched Fartman's huge bulge. I'm not sure if he did that "for power" or just for some cheap thrill, but he did it just the same, on live television. After Fartman stole all of the thunder from Metallica and the entire rest of the show, they hoisted him back up to the rafters while he released his farewell barrage of noisy butt blasts.

But Fartman was at the MTV Awards to do more than present an award to a heavy metal group. He was also there to promote his new movie, which very well might have been called

The Adventures of Fartman. (On his radio show, Howard revealed his "formula" for big-screen success: "My bare ass" plus "nude girls" equal "big bucks.") This was the picture that Howard Stern had signed to do with New Line Cinema, a very respectable movie studio that is best known for its *Teenage Mutant Ninja Turtles* and *Nightmare on Elm Street* films.

Unfortunately, New Line Cinema seemed to have lost its senses, because it demanded that Howard (yes, the same Howard Stern who brought us "Lesbian Dial-a-Date," "Butt Bongo Fiesta," "Tribute to the Vagina") bring the movie in at a rating of PG-13. What the hell could these morons have been thinking? Did they all sit around and think "Jeez, how could we do something so idiotic that it would make the old management of WNBC radio look like geniuses?" What possible explanation could they have had for demanding a PG-13 rating from the man who had a guest light his penis on fire on one of his videos and who frequently asks guests if they are "blond all over"?

Because of New Line's demand that the movie have a PG-13 rating, along with a dispute over merchandising, Howard decided to look elsewhere. Stern is now saying that Fartman will not be his first movie and that he is looking at other script possibilities. Either way, Howard has made it clear, "I'm not going to put out some lame-ass movie." (Interestingly enough, Howard made his movie debut in a lame-ass movie called *Ryder P.I.* In that 1986 film he had a bit role playing a TV anchorman named "Ben-Wah.")

Nonetheless, I am sure that Howard will find a studio that understands his brand of humor better than New Line Cinema. Actually, if I was an employee of New Line Cinema, I would be watching the sky very carefully during the next year or two, because you never know when that BM bomber from the planet "Sphinkton" might just happen to fly overhead and let loose with a Hiroshima-sized breakage of wind. Remember, he is Fartman, and you may be seeing him trouser coughing soon in a theater near you.

14 CHAPTER

SPORTS— FROM TOUCHDOWNS TO RUBDOWNS

Sports has become an increasingly large part of the Stern shows. I think the thing that opened Howard up a lot more to the world of sports was the success of the New York Giants football team in the mid-'80s. It was hard for Howard to ignore the wave of excitement that swept the New York/New Jersey area when the Giants suddenly became a football power to be reckoned with. It was during this time that Leonard Marshall, the great Giant lineman who is now with the Jets, started reporting in to Howard on Mondays about the previous day's Giants game. This

Howard is not above making a wager or two during Super Bowl Sunday. In 1993, some group, in order to bring attention to the problem of spouse abuse, was tracking the number of women who would end up getting beaten during the game. Howard, being in a wagering mood, decided to bet Fred on the number of women beaten. Fred decided to put his money on the "under 720" figure as he stated, "I've got the feeling that it's going to be an exciting game this year, so beatings will be down." Howard, who went with "over 720" beatings, said, "I might actually have to beat my wife to get in on the over/under." Poor Alison.

even led to a bet with the big lineman that Howard would kiss Leonard's "big black ass" in public—right on New York City's Madison Avenue—if the Giants won the Super Bowl. Well, the Giants did win the Super Bowl, and Howard paid his bet in full.

Howard's idea of sports is not getting sweaty and dirty with a bunch of guys; it is getting a massage, or having cherries eaten off your body by a beautiful, topless girl. That is exactly what Howard does each year at the annual Super Bowl Party. Actually, the first few parties were private affairs which Howard just talked about on the air the following Monday. It was during one of these Monday-morning-after sessions that we learned Jackie had stuck his finger up some guy's butt at the party.

The last couple of years have seen the parties move directly onto the airwaves. In 1992, Howard decided to call his wife and assert his divine right to be a man during Super Bowl week. Alison decided to assert her rights as a wife and declared, "I am disgusted by this." Howard did not back down, though, as he described to her how a girl was right at the moment eating a cherry off his buttocks. This proceeded to make Alison extremely pissed, and she stated, "You're disgusting; good-bye!" and hung up.

Well, I guess they figured that the conversation with Alison had gone so well that they decided to give Jackie's wife, Nancy, a call. Nancy was even more upset, and threatened to cut Jackie off in the sex department. "I'll talk to you in about two weeks, Jack," she told her portly, naked husband as she slammed down the receiver. (We found out who wears the pants in Jackie's marriage the following year, as he was not allowed to and did not participate in the 1993 Super Bowl Party. Jackie, you wuss, you might as well just wear a dress to work.)

Football is not the only sport that captures the attention of a great athlete like Howard Stern. First among the others is tennis. Everyone by now knows that the "U.S. Open Sores" video featured Howard and Gary playing a tennis match in front of a sold-out Nassau Coliseum. These guys were definitely not the

Geraldo Rivera—out of his boxing gear—attending a benefit for Hispanic rights. (Brett Lee/Star File)

second coming of Jimmy Connors and John McEnroe; the two of them together probably couldn't beat a dead Arthur Ashe. It had to be quite embarrassing for Howard to lose to the roly-poly producer.

If the tennis loss to Gary was an embarrassment, then Howard should still be hiding his head in complete shame over his basketball game with musician Nils Lofgren. Nils, a "fidget" who can't be much taller than Herve Villechaize ("the plane, the plane"), completely destroyed the 6 foot, 5 inch geeky radio DJ in a televised game of one-on-one. Nils dribbled around Howard like Stern had been standing there when they laid the foundation for the building.

Howard is a better judge of basketball talent than he is a basketball player (hell, he couldn't be any worse). He successfully predicted that Chicago would knock off the red-hot New York Knicks in the 1993 NBA playoffs. He also said that Michael Jordan could have been "the greatest chain stealer who ever lived" if he hadn't chosen basketball as a profession.

If Howard were a sports professional, I think he would be best as a color commentator. This is the role he played during the big boxing match between Geraldo Rivera and Frank Stallone. Yes, the "Scrapple in the Apple" (Robin came up with this name, for you trivia freaks) was one of the most exciting sporting events of the century. Howard pulled no punches with this event, as he even brought in famed boxing great Jake LaMotta to do a prefight analysis. As a bonus, we learned that the rumors about Mr. LaMotta abstaining from sex before a big fight were absolutely true.

Part of the prefight analysis between Howard and Jake focused on each fighter's motivation. Howard asked the champ this about Geraldo: "Jake, would you say a man who has had sex with Bette Midler is pretty angry and probably has an advantage?" Jake, obviously in a Bette-bashing mood, answered that a man would have to be "pretty desperate." The fight went the distance, but there was no doubt that Frank had spanked the cocky Rivera. "I don't get knocked down" was Geraldo's comment to Howard after the fight, but it was clear that he does get beat up.

The other contest that evening was a real pants rippler, "Lesbian Oil Wrestling." During the prefight analysis, Howard said to Jake LaMotta, "Both women could be having their period. How much does that effect a fight, Mr. LaMotta?" Surprisingly enough, Jake didn't really know. I guess the great fighters like Frazier, Ali, Louis, and LaMotta didn't worry about such things before the big fights. The "tale of the tape" in this fight really favored the fighter known as "Tammy" much more than her opponent, "Amy." It was not so much the height and reach advantage, but Tammy's "length of tongue" was a full three-quarters of an inch longer, and she was "butch" while Amy was "fem."

Oh yes, Stern and sports go together like . . . well, like Michael Jackson and girls.

THE PART

HOWARD AND FRIENDS: A VERY INTERESTING CAST OF CHARACTERS

MUSICAL ACCOMPLICES

Now begins a "Who's Who" of the Stern world. These are the people or groups who are either Stern guest celebrities, frequent noncelebrity regulars, or vocal Stern haters. I obviously could not cover everyone whom Howard has had on his show over the past decade, so I have selected the most outstanding. Let's start our journey into the "Who's Who" of Howard Stern with the world of music. Although Howard does not normally play music on his show, he is quite involved in the music world, especially rock 'n' roll. When the Stern show reported that Pete Townshend of the Who had allegedly declared his homosexuality, Stuttering John was really taken aback, and said, "Now when he sings, 'Let My Love Open the Door,' we know what he's talking about."

Howard and crew do not just report on the world of music; some of the industry's top names make frequent appearances on his various radio and television shows. Howard is amazingly adept at talking them into performing some of their hits for the audience, at some god-awful hour of the morning and without any preparation whatsoever. He has many admirers and friends from the rock and roll world. One of the first was Dee Snyder.

DEE SNYDER

Most famous gig: Lead singer for the rock band Twisted Sister.

The first meeting between Dee and Howard was a tense one. Howard apparently had been "bad-rapping" Dee on the radio when Dee confronted him in the "green room" where the guest wait before going on stage, at the Letterman show. Dee stated that he began "cursing" Howard, and the next thing he knew "we became friends."

Howard and Dee would seem to be made for each other. Just how similar is Dee's background to Howard's? Dee was raised on Long Island (as was Howard). Dee felt that he was an "outcast" and "misfit" in school (Howard felt similarly through high school and at Boston University). Both Howard and Dee feel that their parents are mainly responsible for the problems they had growing up. On top of all this, both Dee and Howard have had to fight battles against government types who've wanted to censor their artistic creations. Howard's battle with the FCC is legendary, but many of you may not know that Dee became a "leading spokesman" for freedom of speech in rock 'n' roll when a group of congressmen's wives proclaimed that some of the lyrics sung by Twisted Sister and other groups were "antisocial."

Dee, who now lives in Florida, is also the man responsible for the look and image that Howard has today. Before Dee talked Howard into the "biker/rocker" haircut and clothes, Howard sort of looked like an accountant with a mustache and a bad haircut. Howard, who now seems confused about his new look, once stated, "Am I a biker? I don't even know how to ride a motorcycle."

Dee used to appear regularly on the radio show, but took a five-year hiatus. A few years back, he made a memorable appearance with Howard (which is immortalized on "Crucified by the FCC") in which he traveled down into the "homo room" with Howard and another DJ. There the experimental threesome began opening bottles with their butts. When one broke, Dee stated, "Let's ask a gerbil to push out the cap." Next, the threesome needed to

Stern pal Dee Snyder, 1986. (David Seelig/Star File)

decide whether they wanted to play "penis Ping-Pong" or have "boner fights." (Dee: "Boner fights are my long suit.") The boys decided to go with "penis Ping-Pong" and Dee, again boasting about his size, stated, "Is it fair? My paddle is bigger." Dee, however, lost, as his paddle went prematurely flaccid.

Twisted Sister, whose biggest hit was the loud and very popular "We're Not Gonna Take It," had disbanded. Dee is now a member of a new group, Widow Maker, and has released an album entitled "Blood and Bullets."

Leslie West and company during the heyday of Mountain.

LESLIE WEST

Most famous gig: Lead guitar player for the rock band Mountain.

Leslie is the very large guitar player who rocked us all with great hits like "Mississippi Queen," which has now become the theme song for a beer commercial. He once put out a solo album called "The Great Fatsby." Leslie used to call the Stern show frequently; today he does so less often. He once performed for Howard and fans over the phone, and performed well. He was also an on-again, off-again friend of Sam Kinison's. They had a falling-out when Sam accused Leslie of being the only performer to demand money for his appearance at a benefit for Lenny Bruce's mother.

JOE WALSH

Most famous gig: Guitar player with the Eagles and his own solo career.

Joe is another big fan of Howard's, and used to make frequent appearances on the radio show. Joe would do just about anything Howard asked and often would sing and play some of his biggest hits at a moment's notice. One of my all-time favorite songs is a solo Joe Walsh tune, "Life's Been Good."

Every time Joe appears on the show, it seems as if he is totally wasted. Over the years I have come to realize that this does not necessarily mean he is. I think Joe's normal persona is that of a guy who has drunk five or six too many. Joe's frequent appearances on the Stern show actually led to a brief stint as a DJ for K-Rock. I have to admit that I was very upset to see one of America's greatest rock legends spinning records; it sort of reinforced for me the current belief that rock is dead. Let's face it, if you're not into heavy metal or rap music, your choices are limited to a few good groups like Ugly Kid Joe or 4 Non Blondes, or "classic rock" like Joe Walsh and Eagles tunes. Joe, who started his career as a rock legend with the James Gang, is one of the all-time best Howard guests and should be extended an open invitation to appear. He never disappoints.

Joe Walsh performing at the China Club in Manhattan. (Dominick Conde/Star File)

YOUNG MC

Most famous gig: Solo career as a rap artist.

Young MC was a frequent caller and guest on the Stern radio show. He was also featured on an episode of *The Howard Stern Show* on television, as he and comedian Pat Cooper were

Rap star Young MC. (Al Pereira/Star File)

the main competitors during the "Howard Stern Celebrity Bowling and Christmas Special." He also claimed on Howard's radio show that he slept with *Penthouse* centerfold and frequent Stern guest Amy Lynn. She denied it.

Young MC, who had a big hit with "Bust a Move," got his start by writing for rapper Tone-Loc. He broke out big on his own with the 1989 album "Stone Cold Rhymin'." He is one of the few black celebrities, other than those from the sports arena, who will actually admit to the fact that they like Howard. Sometimes he will try to go toe-to-toe in the verbal ring with Howard but, like everyone else who attempts it, he is usually put facedown on the canvas. He is also the guy who once said he thought Howard was funny except that he sometimes goes too far with the black jokes.

When Young MC informed Howard that his friends told him Howard was a racist, Howard directed him to "stop talking to black people." Howard likes to lump Young MC with "nice" blacks like Sinbad. He even told MC once, "You make Gary Coleman look like a head-hunter."

CHER

Most famous gig: Her infomercials. Oh yeah—she also has a singing and movie career that some of you may be aware of.

Well, I never ever stated that all celebrities appreciate the humor and wit of Mr. Stern. Cher pretty much detests everything about Howard. At least that is the gist of what she said about him in an interview she gave to *TV Guide*. "I hate him. There's no way I could watch him. I have a personal investment in not watching him—he's just a creep." Well, that said a mouthful, didn't it?

Cher was apparently not very happy about the fact that Howard had made fun of her onetime boyfriend, the famous bagel maker Rob Camilletti. "He really attacked Robert and Robert's family, and our relationship," Cher stated.

Well, Cher, I heard a lot of the bits that Howard used to do regarding you and Rob, and I must say, aren't we just a little bit sensitive? As a matter of fact, wasn't it Rob himself who appeared as a mystery guest on the Stern radio show, and he seemed to have a pretty good sense of humor about the whole thing.

I think it's pretty strange that Cher didn't give one specific example of something Howard said that got her upset. She talked about all the "horrible things" that he said about her, but no one's quite sure what she was referring to. You have to wonder if she didn't get a lot of her information about what Howard says secondhand, and if it didn't get embellished in the translation. I think that happens a lot; many stars come on and claim that Howard has been bad-mouthing them, yet cannot be specific about his remarks.

I'm not about to say that Howard didn't poke fun at either Rob or anyone else connected with Cher or at Cher herself. I know for a fact that he has, but he pokes fun at everyone, and Cher certainly is a prime target to be poked fun at. Christ, how could anyone not take a potshot at those damn infomercials she does? Really, Cher, I'm dying to know: Why? It can't be for the money, can it?

Anyway, I heard the Rob Camilletti "bagel boy" imitations and bits and thought they were very funny, but certainly not malicious. I'm not sure what Cher was referring to when she stated, "If someone said that to your girlfriend or your wife, you'd take a gun and shoot him." Having once been married to Sonny Bono, shouldn't she have a better sense of humor?

ENUFF Z'NUFF

Most famous gig: Stern's favorite up-and-coming rock band.

Any regular listener of the Stern radio show will be able to tell you who Enuff Z'Nuff is, but I'm not sure the rest of the world knows. This is a rock band that Howard has taken under his wing, much in the same way he did with Bon Jovi before that group hit it big. Lead singer Chip Z'Nuff and the group were virtual unknowns when Howard let them come on to promote their first album, "Enuff Z'Nuff." Chip and the rest of the band seem good-natured enough, and they do have some great hard-rock songs, such as "Kiss the Clown" and "Fly High Michelle." Enuff Z'Nuff's visits to the K-Rock studio are the best time to find out just how much sex a rock star gets.

THE RAMONES

Most famous gig: Great punk rock band!

Rolling Stone called this band "four scruffy ex–juvenile delinquents from Queens, New York," and the magazine was complimenting them. Here is a group with about twenty years together and fourteen albums to its credit that doesn't get the recognition it deserves for being a fine rock band. It has a great sense of humor, with songs like "Blitzkrieg Bop," and "Bonzo goes to Bitburg." They also make great music, with "I Wanna Be Sedated" one of my all-time favorites.

Joey Ramone in particular is known for his Stern appearances, and could be seen on both the "Celebrity Bowling and Christmas Special" and "Tribute to Breasts" episode of the WWOR-TV show. Many people even say Howard *looks* like

Joey. Just to point out what a happening group this was, they once talked a reporter into believing that the name for their group came about because all of the unrelated members of the band just coincidentally had the same surname.

"PAPA" JOHN PHILLIPS

Most famous gig: Singer and songwriter for the Mamas and the Papas.

Howard look-alike Joey Ramone.
(Gin Satoh/Star File)

"Papa" John is another one of my favorite guests on the radio show. Not only will he always indulge Howard and his fans and sing some of the Mamas and the Papas' greatest hits, but he will talk about anything. This includes his years with the group, the drugs and sex, and his famous daughters. (Mackenzie was, of course, one of the stars of *One Day at a Time*. Chynna is the pretty blond and member of the all-girls group Wilson Phillips.)

Papa John is a musical genius and has led one of the most interesting lives imaginable. Even though he admits to having taken massive amounts of drugs in his younger years, the man can still create good music. I remember a 1989 appearance on the radio show when he decided to play a new song he had just written, "Kokomo." I got the feeling that Howard didn't care for the song much and probably felt that Papa John had little chance of turning it into a hit. Papa John proved once again that he still has it, though, as "Kokomo" became a huge hit for none other than the Beach Boys, who had been pretty dormant at the time.

PIG VOMIT

Most famous gig: Being "Howard Stern's Band."

This is the group that does the playing on a lot of the song parodies that Howard puts together. It backed up Sam Kinison when he performed "Wild Thing" on the "U.S. Open Sores" video. Howard talked briefly to one of the members of the band backstage at that event. If you live in the New York/New Jersey area, you can catch Pig Vomit at various small clubs. It was playing at a small club called the Sports Authority in Rochelle Park, New Jersey, as late as June of 1993, thus proving that it had a long way to go before hitting the big time. In an attempt to capitalize on his name (who doesn't, right, Howard?), Pig Vomit bills itself as "Howard Stern's Band."

BON JOVI

Most famous gig: Pissing off Howard Stern, being used as bait in the Sam Kinison scam, making up with Howard Stern, and selling some records.

As I stated earlier in this book, I am not particularly fond of these guys, or their music. Even though Howard had made peace with them, I think that any true Stern fan still finds them very distasteful. They exemplify the concept of the "fair-weather friend."

Let's review: Before these guys hit the big time, Howard took them in and promoted their careers for them and they became friends. After they became megastars, they began to distance themselves from Howard and didn't come into the radio studio anymore. When Howard would get them on the phone, they would blame it on their record company. When Howard got particularly upset with them for not making an in-studio appearance, guitar player Richie Sambora told him, "Why don't you just lighten up and have some fun, bud?" By this time they were more popular than sex and should have had enough balls to stand up to the record company. What was the record company going to do? It certainly couldn't fire Bon Jovi.

Unfortunately, the feud between Howard and Bon Jovi led

Rock 'n' roll rebels? Jon Bon Jovi and Richie Sambora. (Chuck Pulin/Star File)

to the brief falling-out between Sam Kinison and Howard. Sam, in what had to be his lowest moment, decided to tell Howard that he was going to reunite Howard and Bon Jovi by bringing the group into the K-Rock studio the day after Sam had made an appearance. As everyone knows, the much-awaited and bally-hooed Howard–Bon Jovi reunion never occurred, and led to what was probably the greatest radio in history, the Sam-and-Howard feud. (See Chapter 7 to relive it!)

I'm not sure why Howard would want to make up after all this, but he and Bon Jovi did mend things. The man whom Howard once called "a pussy" and "a jerk," Jon Bon Jovi, began making appearances on the Stern show. Jon and his group appeared via satellite to give out an award on an episode of *The Howard Stern Show* on TV, and Jon appeared with Richie Sambora on *The Howard Stern Interview*. My feeling is that someone connected with the group realized that Howard Stern's popularity was on the way up while Bon Jovi's was heading in the opposite direction.

The entire interview on the E! Channel focused on the fact that Richie Sambora had dated Cher. We learned that it took Richie "a couple of months" to get Cher into bed, that he "couldn't believe" that she actually liked him, and that they made love "many times" in one night. The kicker was when Howard asked Richie, "Do you think about Sonny when you're having sex with her?"

This was the one interview that I must take Howard to task for, as I tuned in expecting to hear how Bon Jovi would explain to Howard why it had ducked him for so many years; but besides one brief reference by Howard to how he had "supported" the group in its early years, the topic was never raised. Howard, you don't need these guys. As a matter of fact, your fans don't listen to their music (they sing songs for the teen girls of the world), and we don't forget that they screwed you for all those years. So Howard, don't waste your time with them; we would rather see a Joe Walsh interview any day.

PATTY SMYTH

Most famous gig: Lead vocalist for the rock band Scandal. Subsequent solo career.

I purposely had Ms. Smyth follow Bon Jovi in this section of the book, as Ms. Smyth is a musician who appreciates what Howard does for people such as herself. Patty called Howard and gave him some of the credit for helping her hit single, "Sometimes Love Just Ain't Enough," climb the charts. Patty's manager, Randy Phillips, was quoted in *Billboard* magazine as saying, "With that kind of audience share there's no question that if she goes on and the song is played, you're going to see some results." Hmmm, I wonder if Bon Jovi's record company has read that?

Patty is not only an appreciative Stern guest, but is also a great singer who's great looking. She had two big hits while with Scandal, "Goodbye to You" and "The Warrior." She also had solo success with "No Mistakes in Love."

During a recent appearance on *The Howard Stern Interview*, Patty was the recipient of Stern's favorite pickup line: "My wife was in a terrible car accident. She's disfigured and she's dead." He went on to tell her what a great mother she would make for his children. One thing we learned about Patty during the interview was that she had been asked by Eddie Van Halen to replace David Lee Roth as lead singer of Van Halen before the group went out and got Sammy Hagar. Believe it our not, she turned the offer down. Good thing she's cute.

STING

Most famous gig: Solo career and being lead singer for the Police.

You know you're a big star when everyone knows you by one name (see Cher). Yet Sting is not too big to have some fun with Mr. Stern. He has sung live on the Stern show and has listened to Howard tell him that his wife is "a real piece of ass" and that he wouldn't mind having sex with her. Howard was slightly miffed after Sting blew him off at a Rock and Roll Hall of Fame event. But this "feud" didn't last long, because Sting called in to the show soon after to make up for the oversight.

ZEROS

Most famous gig: Creating a Stern theme song.

If you have never heard of the Zeros, relax; neither has most of the rest of the world. However, they were responsible for releasing a theme song that Howard used during his days at WNBC. It was aptly titled, "H-O-W-A-R-D." Howard used the song as an opener until the Zeros allegedly began demanding payment for its use. According to a spokesman for the record company that is releasing the Zeros album containing the song, the group became upset that Pig Vomit was playing it in clubs in the New York area.

Last July, the band members made an appearance on the Stern show in which they talked about the "falling-out" and debuted a new version of the song. Although the band wanted to get Howard to once again use the song on a regular basis, he seemed wary about doing so, considering past problems. But Howard did admit he really liked the song, and stated, "I'm thinking this could be our sign-off song." Howard apparently decided against it. For those of you wanting to hear the song, it was released by Restless Records on a five-song set, with "H-O-W-A-R-D" the title number.

TOM JONES

Most famous gig: Solo career.

Mr. Jones has been interviewed by Howard on both the radio and the E! TV show. Howard said to him, "You have a big package in your pants." Tom told Howard that Milton Berle, who is legendary in the penis department, once came up to Tom and showed him his penis. Howard asked Tom, "Did it take your breath away?" Tom answered, "It did," and admitted that it was bigger than his, but not by a whole lot. Amazingly, not once in all the years Johnny Carson hosted *The Tonight Show* did he find out one guest's penis size. It took Howard less than a full season to find out that Tom Jones is hung like a horse, yet is still smaller than Milton Berle.

PETER NOONE

Most famous gig: Lead singer of rock band Herman's Hermits.

Another really cool older rocker. His hit songs include "I'm Henry the Eighth, I Am," and "Mrs. Brown, You've Got a Lovely Daughter." Howard turned the latter hit into "Don't You Dare Have Lunch With Jeffrey Dahmer," which Peter was nice enough to sing on the show. With lines in the song like "He'll cut off your privates and make penis pie" and "Too bad he didn't hack off both of Pee Wee's arms," it is obvious that Peter has quite a sense of humor. We also learned during one of Peter's visits that he had been trying to have a child for eighteen years before he finally was successful. This led Howard to spout off his classic line: "Herman wasn't spermin', but he is now."

TOP FIVE MUSICIANS WHO "REFUSED" TO APPEAR ON HOWARD'S WWOR-TV SHOW

●1●
Frank Sinatra

●2●
Eric Clapton

●3●
Kenny Rogers

●4●
Dolly Parton

●5●
Heavy D

16 CHAPTER

COMEDIC COLLEAGUES

After musicians, the next most frequent category of celebrity that Howard gets to appear on his shows would have to be comedians. His guests have ranged from Bob Hope and Milton Berle to Sam Kinison and Andrew "Dice" Clay. No matter who it is or what generation he or she is from, Howard manages to make the most out of each comic's appearance. Sam Kinison remains Howard's best guest ever, which is why he deserved his own chapter (see Chapter 7). Here are some of the other comedy-related guests; but keep in mind that it was impossible to include more than a small number of the memorable comics who have appeared with Stern.

GARY SHANDLING

Most famous gig: Star of *It's Gary Shandling's Show* and *The Larry Sanders Show*.

Gary gets prime placement as the first comedian in this chapter not because he is the most frequent Stern guest or even one of Stern's best guests, but because he was the guy who had the balls to be the first guest on *The Howard Stern Interview*.

I must admit, Howard's first interview on the E! Channel was more like a twenty-minute commercial for himself. At one point he asked Gary to "evaluate this interview on a scale from one to ten." Gary responded, "I'll let you know when I start participating." At the end of the interview, Gary stated that he didn't think it was "as bad as I thought it was going to be." When Howard asked him what he expected, he answered, "Hell." Howard returned the favor and appeared on Gary's *Larry Sanders Show*.

ANDREW "DICE" CLAY

Most famous gig: Profane stand-up routine. Star of the mediocre movie *The Adventures of Ford Fairlane*.

Poor Andrew Clay Silverstein (his real name)—he's sort of the Rodney Dangerfield of the 1990s. This comedian is constantly bad-mouthed by everyone, including other comedians. The only person who comes to his defense seems to be Howard Stern, and even Howard has his problems with the "Dice Man."

Personally, I think Andrew "Dice" Clay came up with a very funny, original, and filthy stand-up routine that I'm sure was offensive to some people. Hey, people shouldn't listen to his act if they find him offensive. I thought I would bust a gut the first time I heard him tell how he was standing on line at a bank "with my tongue stuck up some chick's ass," but that's just my incredibly sick sense of humor acting up again. My problem with Mr. Clay is that he never developed anything funny after that original comic routine. His movie wasn't really funny and he never developed past his dirty nursery rhyme stage.

The other major problem encountered by Mr. Clay, especially as it concerns the Stern show, was the fact that he is nowhere near as funny as the late, great Sam Kinison. It's not as if he deserves the comparison, either, but he helped bring it on himself with the feud that the two used to play out on the airwaves when either one would appear with Howard. (One time Dice came on and told how his sidekick, "Hot Tub Johnny," took the "do rag" [bandanna] off Sam's head and kicked his butt.)

There was this competition thing between the two that Howard seemed to encourage, but it was not a fair competition at all. The difference between Sam and Dice is like night and day. Sam had a quick comedic mind that could be funny on a moment's notice,

Overrated Stern guest Andrew "Dice" Clay. (David Seelig/Star File)

even if the mind happened to be under the influence of some mind-altering drug. Dice, on the other hand, is rarely funny when he visits the Stern studio. He's not quick or witty; as a matter of fact, if you take him away from some prewritten or scripted material, forget it. He's probably one of the worst studio guests Howard has ever had on the show.

One of the most ironic things that came out of the Dice Man's talk show romps was his tiff with Arsenio Hall. This led to his appearance on an episode of the Stern TV show in which he proceeded to call Arsenio a "ghetto-blasting . . . Jessie

Jackson-ass-kissing, saliva-spraying, fart-laying, waitress-stiffing ... nose-picking, butt-stinking, Richard Pryor-mimicking ... Colt 45-drinking, skirt-chasing ... future busboy." Why do I get the feeling that the Dice Man is correct about Arsenio as a "future busboy"? But for some reason I picture Arsenio dumping the plates he cleans up into a sinkful of soapy water, and then an old guy in a leather jacket and apron, a cigarette hanging out of the corner of his mouth and a name tag that says "Andy" on his chest, washing those plates.

Comedian Richard Belzer, otherwise known as "The Belz."

RICHARD BELZER

Most famous gig: Stand-up act. Actor.

Richard Belzer has made numerous appearances on the radio show and even appeared on Howard's first video, the "Underpants and Negligee Party," as a judge on the "Star Search" segment. I want to be able to like Richard Belzer, but I don't. It is something that started when I first began listening to Howard's radio show. "The Belz" would come on and treat Howard like shit. He constantly gave the impression that he thought he was too good to be doing Howard's show and that he resented being there. I'm never quite sure why Howard put up with him in those earlier years.

Belzer has begun to lighten up, but he used to get pretty

irritated at Howard for harping on the fact that Belzer has only one testicle. (Belzer was diagnosed as having cancer in 1984 and underwent an operation and radiation treatment.) The other topic that Howard loves to discuss, much to Belzer's chagrin, is that he is married to actress Harlee McBride, who starred in the soft-porn (i.e., no penetration) movies *Young Lady Chatterly* and *Young Lady Chatterly II*.

GILBERT GOTTFRIED

Super Stern guest Gilbert Gottfried at the MTV Awards. (Bob Gruen/Star File)

Most famous gig: Stand-up act. Bit parts in movies.

Gilbert is another comic who has numerous appearances on the Stern radio show to his credit. I think Howard should start a club, like "The Fifty-Appearance Club," and give out a pin or something to commemorate when a guest becomes a member. Gilbert would be especially deserving, because he is funny every single time he comes on the show. He is also one of the guests who inspires Howard to outdo himself (Sam did this also). Whether placing phony phone calls, doing Jerry Seinfeld impressions, or just commenting on the news, Howard and Gilbert always make for a lively show.

PAT COOPER

Most famous gig: Stand-up act. Stern radio appearances.

Pat is an old-time comic who would never kiss anyone's ass, and although he might not have any regrets, I think even he would admit that it hurt his career. Pat hasn't changed a lot. He seems angry with the world.

On what has to be one of the top ten Stern radio moments,

TOP TEN BEST AND WORST GUESTS

Top Ten Best Stern Guests		Top Ten Worst Stern Guests
Sam Kinison	-1-	Jon Bon Jovi
Jessica Hahn	-2-	Dennis Miller
Richard Simmons	-3-	Emo Phillips
Gilbert Gottfried	-4-	Young MC
Joan Rivers	-5-	Andrew "Dice" Clay
Pat Cooper	-6-	Dick Cavett
Geraldo Rivera	-7-	Richard Marx
Meg Griffin	-8-	Tony Bennett
Joe Walsh	-9-	Steve Rossi
Sandra Bernhard	-10-	Richard Lewis

Pat Cooper had a knock-down, nasty, verbal radio fight with his family, including his mother and his son. It was during the father-son portion of the dispute that Howard thought he had his best chance of actually bringing two family members back together. When he finally talked Pat into saying, "Mike, I love you" to his son, it looked like a tearful reunion was a lock. However, when Pat's son responded, "I never heard that before," Pat answered back with, "You may never hear it again." I was

Mr. Family Man, Pat Cooper.

never quite sure who disowned whom, but I am certain that *The Waltons* was not based on any part of Pat Cooper's family.

Of course, I couldn't go without mentioning the confrontation between rapper Young MC and Pat. Pat was very upset that Young MC had known all about the Milli Vanilli lip-synching scam but had not come forward and told anyone until after the story broke. (Young MC had opened for Milli Vanilli on an early tour.) Pat was pretty blunt with Young MC, considering he had never even met the man at the time. "You ain't got balls" and "You have no character" were just a couple of the insults Pat threw at Young MC, who was taking heat from both Howard and Pat.

With the two of them backing Young MC into a corner, he tried to battle back with "I want you to eat me raw" and "Why don't you say it with your teeth in, you son of a bitch," but by that time, Young MC had been pretty well dissed. This dispute was later settled at the bowling alley on an episode of *The Howard Stern Show* on TV, with Young MC proving that he bowls about as well as he argues.

The Petite Flower," Judy Tenuta, at the Palladium in New York City. (Chuck Pulin/Star File)

JUDY TENUTA

Most famous gig: Stand-up act.

Judy is the very loud, gypsy-looking, accordion-playing comedienne who likes to let men know that we are all her "love slaves." She is a good Stern guest and Howard loves to set her up. Once she ran out of the studio, almost in tears, when Howard, Sam, and some others all ganged up on her. She also believes that Roseanne Arnold stole a lot of her routine. On one visit to the Stern radio show, Howard prepped callers before Judy came on to tell her how much better a comedienne Roseanne is. One caller was really giving it to Judy when she lost control. "Listen, pig, she used to watch me all the time," Judy screamed. When the guy kept at her, she yelled for Howard to turn off the "fucking pig." Howard bleeped it in time.

It took Howard quite a few visits by Judy to learn that she and fellow comedian Emo Phillips were actually an item. It seemed to be something the two wanted to hide, but Howard always gets to the bottom of things. Still, it's hard to believe that Emo plays the role of "stud puppet" to the "Love Goddess."

CHEVY CHASE

Most famous gig: An original "Not Ready for Prime Time Player" on *Saturday Night Live*. Actor. Former talk show host.

Chevy was great during his one year of *Saturday Night Live*. He was super in *Caddyshack*, *National Lampoon's*

Vacation, and other films. Unfortunately, Chevy got involved in a bit of a "pissing contest" with Howard that has made him look like a chump. It all started when Howard called Chevy at his house and, according to Chevy, "bullied" his maid into putting Chevy on the phone. From there things got way out of hand. First, in a heated phone conversation, Chevy told Howard, "Do you know what a bully is? I don't like bullies. Is that clear? I don't like people calling my home early in the morning and I don't like you, period."

Well, apparently Chevy doesn't know Howard very well, because he would have realized that Howard doesn't let anyone off the hook quite that easily. Very soon after the telephone conversation with Chevy, Howard started playing a "Dear Jesus" spoof which had a little girl's voice asking questions of Chevy like, "Can you make anyone laugh anymore?" and "I heard you used to be famous in 1975," and "Maybe you are mad that you lost your hair." Ouch!

On top of that, Stuttering John tracked Chevy down and asked him, "Do you know what a bully is?" Chevy replied that a bully is "a guy about six foot five who calls up people who can barely speak the language and bullies them over the telephone. . . . That's a bully. . . . A bully's a guy who picks on a guy with a speech impediment until he can hardly speak anymore. . . . That's what a bully is." Well, Chevy, for your information, John could "hardly speak" long before Howard began picking on him, so there.

ELAINE BOOSLER

Most famous gig: Stand-up act. Cable TV special.

Elaine certainly didn't make it into the book based on her talent. She's about as funny as a cemetery. However, she is one of the only comedians who actually caused Howard to be physically attacked. It was on one of the "on-location" shows that Howard periodically does from the Grammys or Oscars, when he decided to find out why Elaine would not come over and talk to him. He began to call out to her over a bullhorn, of course

TOP TEN COMEDIANS WHO "REFUSED" TO APPEAR ON THE WWOR-TV SHOW

1● Sid Caeser
2● Jonathan Winters
3● Bill Cosby
4● Phyllis Diller
5● George Burns
6● Morey Amsterdam
7● Arte Johnson
8● Gabe Kaplan
9● Jimmy Walker
10● Redd Foxx

(Unfortunately, Henny Youngman
has agreed to do the show
before he dies.)

taking a verbal jab at her in the process. The next thing you heard was banging and crashing and people yelling. Robin was heard trying to restore order, and it was finally explained that Elaine's boyfriend-manager had attacked Howard. It made for great radio and was probably the most interesting thing Elaine has ever been responsible for.

GUEST

HOSTS

Let's jump right into what has got to be one of the most interesting categories of Stern guests and nonguests: Talk show and television hosts.

JOAN RIVERS

Most famous gig: Host of *Can We Shop*, *The Joan Rivers Show*, ex–guest host on *The Tonight Show*, stand-up act. Author.

I liked Joan Rivers before she became a regular guest on the *Howard Stern Show* on radio and before she started having Howard on her show, but not half as much as I do now that she has become friends with Howard. To me, she is what comedy is all about. She proved to me that she can take the same type of ribbing that for years she's been handing out. No, that's not true—Howard gives her a much worse ribbing than she ever handed out to anyone, and she always gets a kick out of him.

When Joan appeared on *The Howard Stern Interview*, Howard went over her complete plastic surgery history, inquired about her sex life after Edgar, and called the jewelry that she sells on a cable shopping channel "junk." Joan, who had been through quite a trying period after her Fox television show was canceled and her hus-

Joan Rivers, late husband Edgar Rosenberg, and Spike in New York City. (Vincent Zuffante/Star File)

band, Edgar, committed suicide, did not act the least bit shocked when Howard asked her, "Did Edgar ever tie you up in bed?"

Howard and Joan seem to make magic together whenever Joan appears on his show or Howard appears on hers. One such appearance on her show had Howard coming out and feeling up Joan's butt—on daytime television! Then he berated Joan over a show she had done with her daughter, Melissa.

On that show, Melissa and Joan had both become emotional, causing Howard to ask, "What is her problem with you? . . . I'd love to have you for a mother. . . . The payload you're going to leave that daughter, she should be kissing your feet." Joan explained to Howard that her daughter had been through a lot, with Edgar's suicide and all. Howard got very upset at this and said, "Here I am on a roll, so Joan brings up suicide. Great. . . . Don't say suicide, say you haven't seen your husband in a couple of weeks."

The two went on to talk about Howard's problems with the FCC, and Howard asked, "Joan, what's wrong with penis? . . . Nothing. [Joan] just can't find any." Remember, this was daytime television, and gray-haired housewives all over the country must have been stunned. Finally, in one of those typical talk show stunts, Joan brought out a psychic who wanted a lock of hair from Howard so she could study it. Well, he certainty wasn't going to give her any of the long, curly hair from his head, so he started to pull down his pants, before Joan talked him into just giving up some chest hair.

Another time on Joan's talk show, Howard came out after what had just been a dreadful interview between Joan and David Bowie's ex-wife Angela Bowie. Joan had been told that Angela was ready to reveal all kinds of juicy gossip about David and the rock 'n' roll scene in general, but Angela didn't deliver. When Howard came out and saw how upset Joan was about the interview, he had Joan bring Angela back out.

Unbelievably, it was only minutes before Howard had Angela telling a nationwide television audience how she had once caught David Bowie in bed with Mick Jagger. This revelation received national press coverage, and Angela went on to write a tell-all book about her rock 'n' roll marriage. (Of course, the media never gave Howard the credit he deserved for getting the confession out of her.)

Joan is one of the most good-natured guests you could ever find. Howard once told his audience, "Joan likes it from the back, she told me." If that wasn't bad enough, he added, "Where is Spike [her dog] licking?" Joan is not above giving her own brand of good-natured ribbing back to Howard, once telling him he looked like "Cher on steroids."

However, you can tell that there is a mutual respect and a real fondness between the two of them. During "The Howard Stern Roast," instead of taking a shot at Howard like every other guest did, Joan left this message of love: "I'm glad you're here, I'm glad you're here to stay, and I'm glad we're friends." Classy woman.

JOHNNY CARSON

Most famous gig: Legendary host of *The Tonight Show* for thirty years, now retired.

No, he has never been a guest on any of Howard's shows and no, Howard was never on with Johnny, but Mr. Carson's name sure comes up a lot around Howard. I put Johnny in this spot directly after Joan because, according to Ms. Rivers, Johnny would not give her his blessing when she left to do her own TV show after her guest-host contract with *The Tonight Show* had expired. Not only did he not give her his blessing, but he reportedly hung up on her when she called to tell him about her offer from the Fox network.

In a conversation about this topic with Howard, Joan made it clear that she felt she had been blacklisted from doing David Letterman's show (then *Late Night*) because of Johnny. Howard, upon hearing this, told Joan, "This Johnny Carson is such a creep. I'd rather not be in any kind of career than have to go kiss Johnny's ass."

I think Howard proved his friendship to Joan when he went on *Late Night* and told Letterman, "Now the day has come where all of show business does not have to kiss Johnny Carson's ass anymore. . . . Johnny was a big bore. . . . I never liked Johnny." After Dave told Howard that he does like Johnny, Howard really put him on the spot with "I never liked what he did with Joan Rivers. The idea that you have to ask somebody permission to get a TV show is wrong—don't you think, Dave?" After David tried to wriggle his way out of a conversation which was obviously making him uncomfortable, Howard said, "'Johnny is a big pain in the ass' is what Dave is trying to say."

JAY LENO

Most famous gig: Current host of *The Tonight Show*.

Jay Leno is a great guy and was a frequent caller of the *Howard Stern Show* on radio. He obviously wanted to set his own standard for *The Tonight Show* when he asked Howard

TOP TEN GUEST APPEARANCES ON OTHER PEOPLE'S SHOWS

1. Late night
(David Letterman)
Multiple superb appearances.

2. The Tonight Show
His first appearance is a classic that will never
be matched by any of Jay Leno's future guests. Only
Howard would have the balls to come on and trash Carson
and crew.

3. The Late Show (David Letterman)
One classic book-plugging appearance so far. ("Who's writing
any good books? All nitwits. Another industry I could conquer.")

4. Donahue
Another classic book-plugging appearance, but this one marked by
Howard chasing Phil around the studio so he could give him a kiss.

5. The Arsenio Hall Show
The resulting feud makes this one a classic.

6. The Joan Rivers Show
These two make magic together.

7. The Larry Sanders Show
Very funny appearance by Stern, but he was underused.

8. MTV Awards
Very funny appearance in 1992.

9. Geraldo
Geraldo proved that he's better as a guest on the Stern
show than he is interviewing Howard.

10. Hollywood Squares
Howard replaces Shadoe Stevens in the
bottom center square for a week, but
the censors cut out all of
his best jokes.

Stern to make his first-ever appearance on the king of all talk shows. I really respect Jay for having Howard on so quickly after he took over, and Howard's visit produced the single most entertaining *Tonight Show* ever.

For those of you who did not see this classic appearance by the King of New York (and now Los Angeles), you'd better catch it in a rerun. First of all, fans camped outside *The Tonight Show* studios the night before just to get tickets. That's how popular Howard had become in L.A., even though his show had only recently gone into syndication there. The show was an amazing piece of television history and really ushered *out* the Johnny Carson era on NBC. Even though Howard had to agree that he would not talk about Johnny by name, he was allowed to call Ed McMahon and Doc Severinsen all kinds of names, and really bashed them, especially Ed ("That big fat blubber"), for going on Arsenio and stabbing Jay in the back. Jay sat there and cringed during most of Howard's verbal blasts at the old *Tonight Show* regime, but you could almost tell that he was rooting Howard on and agreeing with most of what he said. (Jay, if I'm wrong about that let me know and I'll be happy to come on your show and apologize personally.) Anyway, Howard was at his best, and even though it may have scared off some of the old-timers who loved Johnny, it had to have helped Jay in the ratings. Now that David Letterman has moved to CBS and is up against Jay's show, the smarter of the two will have Howard on as much as possible.

DAVID LETTERMAN

Most famous gig: Host of *The Late Show*.

The onetime television weatherman has become the best talk show host in the business. Howard's appearances with Letterman are always marked by the outrageous. He is about the only guest I can think of who can actually shock David, and I think that's why David likes him so much. Who else could get away with taking his shoe off and combing David's hair with his foot? David was quoted in *Rolling Stone* as saying, "There are times when [Howard] seems so bright and witty to me, I just think, 'Damn, this guy is blue-chip!'" David goes on to talk about how amazed he is that Howard can get guys to come down on his radio station and "expose themselves" for movie tickets. He adds, "The movie company must be down on their knees giving thanks to God!"

During one of the many Stern appearances on *Late Night*, David told Howard, "You are the cutting edge of show business." Thank you, Mr. Letterman, for being the only entertainment giant with enough balls to say it.

ARSENIO HALL

Most famous gig: Host of *The Arsenio Hall Show*.

Howard's one and only appearance on Fox's late-night show, hosted by Arsenio Hall, ended up with Howard being escorted off the premises before his interview had officially ended. Howard's crime was blaming Fox for the suicide of Edgar Rosenberg. Before he was thrown off, he verbally slapped Johnny Carson for his abuse of Joan Rivers. The funny thing is that Arsenio introduced Howard as "the meanest, nastiest, dirtiest DJ in the whole wide world, my man, Howard Stern." Yet when Howard became just slightly mean, they threw him off the show! I guess Fox can dish it out, but can't take it.

This little episode led to some verbal warfare between Howard and Arsenio, as Howard trashed the black talk show host on an appearance with Letterman. He went so far as to tell David that Arsenio's audience resembled the cast of *Blackula*. Arsenio was soon anointed with the new name by which Stern fans now know him, "Assmoochio." After Howard's *Late Night* stint, Arsenio went on and called Howard "Coward Stern" and told his audience that he couldn't believe how much Howard had kissed David's butt. Robin Quivers called Arsenio "a coward" because he will not come on and talk to Stern and company.

GERALDO RIVERA

Most famous gig: Host of *Geraldo*.

It's hard to believe that Geraldo was once a serious broadcast journalist. With his tabloid talk show and his tell-all book, *Exposing Myself*, I don't think Geraldo will be up for the Peter Jennings anchor desk at ABC anytime soon. On the other hand, Geraldo has probably garnered more fame for himself than Peter Jennings, Tom Brokaw, and Dan Rather combined with things like "Al Capone's Vault," his fistfights with white supremacists, and his allegedly sleeping with Bette Midler and others during his sex addiction days. What I like about Geraldo is that no matter what you think of the guy, he definitely is no pussy. He'll go toe-to-toe with anyone, including Frank Stallone (see Chapter 14).

Frequent butt of Howard's jokes, talk show host Arsenio Hall. (Vincent Zuffante/Star File)

When he was a guest on *The Howard Stern Interview*, Geraldo actually told Howard he was sorry he wrote *Exposing Myself* because so many people got upset over it. However, when Howard mentioned one of the people who was real pissed off about the book, Bette Midler, Geraldo said, "Great Tits." Shocking! Another shocking revelation from the book is that Geraldo says that he would have had homosexual sex

Larry King, one of the many people Howard enjoys making fun of. (Chuck Pulin/Star File)

with Mick Jagger, "if I was so inclined." What the hell does that mean!?

The entire interview was about Geraldo's sex life, past and present, except for the very end. Howard finally got to Geraldo's career, and his very last question was about Oprah Winfrey: "She's a big fat cow, why can't you beat her in the ratings?" Shocking!

LARRY KING

Most famous gig: Host of *Larry King Live* on CNN.

Larry has been a favorite target of the phony phone callers who love to get on the air and shout out something about Howard Stern. Larry hates this, and you really can't blame him, but it's still fun for us Stern fans. Larry is also responsible for what has got to be the lamest newspaper column in the world. His *USA Today* column consists entirely of things like: Is it just me or does everyone eat oatmeal for breakfast? or: In my opinion, there's no finer actor than Larry Storch. What's the deal? Do we really need to know every single thought that runs through Larry King's head? I think most of that column is written when he's on the toilet without a crossword puzzle to do.

One *Larry King Live* takeoff Howard had on the old TV show featured Tawney Kitaen, "Star of the Small Screen" (*WKRP in Cincinnati* and *America's Funniest People*); Sally Kirkland, "Star of the Silver Screen" (a whole host of B movies); and Denise Miller, "Star of Stage." Tawney and Sally were quite unaware that they had been set up by "Larry" (Howard) until after they had told about their experiences in their respective fields.

When it came time for Denise to show off her talents, it was revealed that her stage name is the "Kielbasa Queen," and she demonstrated that her special stage talent is swallowing a twelve-inch kielbasa. The looks on Tawney's and Sally's faces when they realized who they were sharing the stage with was as memorable as seeing the long sausage sucked down the Kielbasa Queens's throat and brought back up again.

The very dapper and very dull Dick Cavett. (Eugene Shaw/Star File)

Larry's only real appearance on the old TV show consisted of a taped message left for Howard during the roast: "You know what I imagine when I envision Howard Stern? A birthday cake . . . He blows out the candles. . . . He wishes he were Larry King." Yeah, I think Howard wants a column where he can tell everyone: Is it just me or do all guys masturbate before they go to sleep each night?

DICK CAVETT

Most famous gig: Host of *The Dick Cavett Show, The Dick Cavett Show, The Dick Cavett Show, The Dick Cavett Show,* and *The Dick Cavett Show.*

You can look at Dick's having five different *Dick Cavett Shows* in one of two ways: Either he is really good and they keep bringing it back, or he is really bad and it keeps getting canceled. Howard is obviously convinced that it is the latter. When Dick appeared on *The Howard Stern Interview*, Howard announced to the audience, "I'm going to attempt to do something tonight that no one else has been able to do: Make Dick Cavett interesting." Besides Richard Simmons, Dick is probably the person whom Howard treats with the most disrespect. But for some reason, Dick keeps coming back for more. Often he will call into the radio station, and Howard will become bored with him and hang up on him in midsentence. Not one to take a hint, Dick will then call him back immediately. You can't blame Howard; when Dick goes off on one of his long-winded tangents, he could get himself kicked out of a leper colony.

MORTON DOWNEY JR.

Most famous gig: Host of *The Morton Downey Jr. Show*.

Morton had a TV show despite having absolutely no talent other than being obnoxious and being able to insult people really well. Apparently he hasn't lost the ability to be obnoxious, as he is the only person to date who has gotten into a fight with Stuttering John over the questions he was being asked. Morton is one of those guys who can dish it out but can't take it. As previously reported, he started a fight with John over a question like "Would your wife go and dance topless in clubs for money if you really needed it?" Yet when he was put on the radio airwaves by Mr. Stern with an ex-employee of his, he called her an "ungrateful bitch" and a "frizzle-haired blonde." He also told her, "You weren't even a blow job, baby," and "You couldn't work your way out of a tiger's butt if you had cleats on." Mort's ex-employee did finally get to spit this out: "You are such an asshole." Hear! Hear!

chapter 18

THESPIANS,
THESPIANS,
THESPIANS

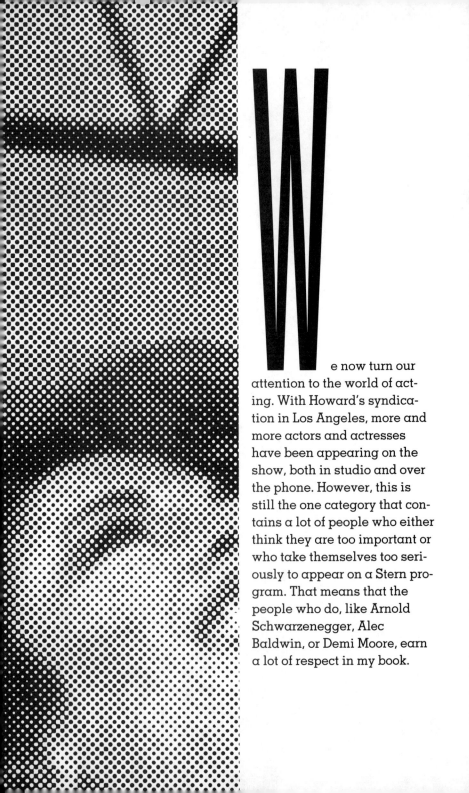

We now turn our attention to the world of acting. With Howard's syndication in Los Angeles, more and more actors and actresses have been appearing on the show, both in studio and over the phone. However, this is still the one category that contains a lot of people who either think they are too important or who take themselves too seriously to appear on a Stern program. That means that the people who do, like Arnold Schwarzenegger, Alec Baldwin, or Demi Moore, earn a lot of respect in my book.

ZSA ZSA GABOR

Most famous gig: Appearing in fifty-seven different films, having eight different husbands, slapping one cop.

Zsa Zsa became friends with Howard during his one-week stint on *Hollywood Squares*. (Yes, Howard was actually on the *Squares*, as a fill-in replacement for Shadoe Stevens. It was a week that saw most of Howard's jokes cut out of the program because they were a bit too risqué for the *Hollywood Squares* audience.) Zsa Zsa was a corner square the same week and

Stern friend Zsa Zsa Gabor. (Vincent Zuffante/Star File)

liked Howard from the start. It's a very strange friendship, but it seems to work. Since their meeting, Zsa Zsa has appeared on both of Howard's television shows. During one of the WWOR shows, she was interviewed by "Johnny Carstern" and had to deal with an Ed McMahon character played by Al Rosenberg, who simply laughed throughout the entire sketch. Ed literally kissed Johnny's bare butt at the end of the bit and after he was finished, his entire nose was covered with shit.

In the meantime, we learned quite a bit about Zsa Zsa, including the fact that she was "madly in love" with Greta Garbo but "didn't know what lesbianism was." When Howard asked her if she prefers "a man's tongue or a woman's," she told him that he was "vulgar." Zsa Zsa went on to tell Howard how Greta Garbo "kissed" her, how she hates Jay Leno because he made jokes about her slapping the cop, and how Johnny Carson was "boring." Not bad for one short interview with a man laughing hysterically in your ear the entire show.

She did even better on *The Howard Stern Show Interview*, in which we found out that she did not consummate her marriage to her latest "Prince" of a husband on her wedding night; that onetime husband George Sanders used to make her "sit up and bark"; and that she feels her sister Eva and Merv Griffin "seriously" love each other. Hey, I like someone who is willing to open up on a talk show. At the end of the interview, Howard planted a huge kiss on her and told everyone that Zsa Zsa was "opening her mouth." Gee whiz, she really *is* willing to open up.

JACKIE STALLONE

Most famous gig: Sylvester Stallone's mother.

Okay, so she isn't actually a movie star. The reason she gets on Howard's radio show is because she is related to one. I wanted to include Jackie because she is another celebrity who had a Pat Cooper-type of appearance on the *Howard Stern Show*. Such appearances are a voyeur's delight. In this one an argument erupted between Jackie and her ex-husband on the phone, and it got about as vicious as any that Howard has had the pleasure of airing. When Jackie's ex called her "the lowest vermin" he has ever known, Jackie freaked. She pounced on him with "Listen, you pig. Let me tell you, you old son of a bitch. You beat me up and put me in the hospital so many times and choked me to death. . . . You never supported your kids. . . . Fuck you. . . . Don't you ever talk to me again, you fucking creep." Seems as if Sly and little brother Frank had quite the home life.

SHARON STONE

Most famous gig: Actress in such films as *Basic Instinct, Total Recall,* and *Sliver.*

Howard told a wonderful story about Ms. Stone on one of his many spectacular *Late Night* appearances with David Letterman.

Apparently, on a previous Letterman visit, Stern had been the guest before Ms. Stone was scheduled to come out and talk to David. During Howard's appearance he talked about how much he enjoyed Sharon in *Basic Instinct* and how turned on he had become during the infamous pantie-less interrogation scene. Howard told David that he was so excited by Ms. Stone in that scene that he "played with himself." According to Howard, Sharon "flipped out" when she heard this and was unwilling to even walk by Stern backstage at *Late Night*, so Letterman's staff tried to usher Howard out the back way, past the garbage, in order for Ms. Stone to avoid seeing him.

Howard, rightly so, became hostile and told them, "I'm a regular on the show. . . . Let that bitch walk out by the garbage." During Howard's story, David sort of sat there and grimaced the entire time; however, Howard made an excellent point. Here is a woman who makes a living by taking her clothes off in movies, yet gets offended when someone admits that they got turned on by her. Well, Ms. Stone, whether you like to face facts or not, you had men all across this country pleasuring themselves over your brilliant acting performances in both *Basic Instinct* and your follow-up, *Sliver*. Keep up the good work and we'll keep up our part of the deal.

HYAPATIA LEE

Most famous gig: Appearing in such adult films as *The Masseuse* and *Indian Summer*.

Hyapatia is here representing all of the adult film stars whom Howard has had on his shows over the years. Hyapatia was actually a spokesmodel on *The Howard Stern Show*, at which time Howard showed a quick clip of *The Masseuse*. Hyapatia, who is part American Indian, told Howard, "My best Indian dancing is on your totem pole." Yikes!

Howard had an encounter with a porn star called Viper that was so graphic that not even Howard would air it (on his radio show). The only place to hear the encounter with the star of such films as *Butt Naked*, *The Hindlick Maneuver*, and *Ass Masters* is on Howard's audiotapes, "Crucified by the FCC." If you haven't heard the tapes and are wondering what possibly could have been so bad that even Howard wouldn't air it, it

"Grampa" Al Lewis partying at the Hard Rock Cafe in New York City. (Chuck Pulin/Star File)

may have something to do with Viper telling Howard about a Pit Bull that was "too short to get his dick in me." Wow, do you really think the FCC would have been upset to hear about a girl and her dog?

AL LEWIS

Most famous gig: Playing "Grampa" on *The Munsters*; writing the Foreword to this book.

A lot of people don't realize that Al Lewis was not only one of the stars of the great TV show *The Munsters*, but starred in *Car 54, Where Are You?*, scouted for the Boston Celtics, and owned a restaurant in New York. Lately, he has become best known for his countless appearances on Howard's radio and WWOR shows, as well as in "U.S. Open Sores" and at the big FCC rally that Howard held in New York.

Al's greatest Stern moment came when he yelled "Fuck the FCC" over and over again during a live broadcast of the Stern radio show at the FCC rally. It was one of the few times that the so-called "Shock Jock" has been shocked. Al Lewis has become the Howard Stern of the geriatric set. He called rapper Young MC "Mandingo" during the "Celebrity Bowling and Christmas Special," which may have contributed to the young black rapper's bowling gutter ball after gutter ball. You also have to respect Al's bravery in going toe-to-toe with Howard in verbal warfare. When Al told Howard "You played like shit" after his tennis match at the Nassau Coliseum, Howard went ballistic on him. "Fuck you, Grampa. Fuck you and your fucking Munsters."

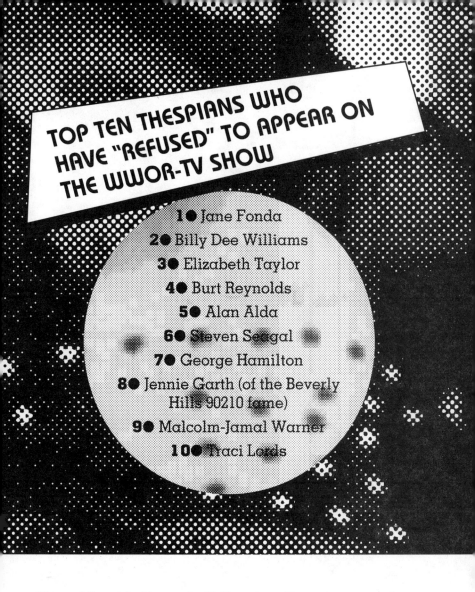

TOP TEN THESPIANS WHO HAVE "REFUSED" TO APPEAR ON THE WWOR-TV SHOW

1 ● Jane Fonda

2 ● Billy Dee Williams

3 ● Elizabeth Taylor

4 ● Burt Reynolds

5 ● Alan Alda

6 ● Steven Seagal

7 ● George Hamilton

8 ● Jennie Garth (of the Beverly Hills 90210 fame)

9 ● Malcolm-Jamal Warner

10 ● Traci Lords

Howard then tried to get the Coliseum audience to turn against Grampa, but this backfired. When Howard asked, "Don't you like the new *Munsters* better?" the audience began to boo in support of "Grampa Al," and for once, Howard lost a round.

19 CHAPTER

CELEBRITIES, FREAKS, AND A JANITOR

Ah, now that we have finished with the people who easily fit into categories, we can get to the fun part. This section covers everyone else who I think has made a memorable appearance or appearances, on the *Howard Stern Show*. Not only true "celebrities" but also those special people who are celebrated by Howard Stern fans alone. Again, I can't include everyone, but here are my favorites. The first person would have a chapter of his own if there were more room in this book. He takes a backseat only to Sam and Jessica when it comes to memorable Stern guest appearances.

Richard Simmons: Won't you come back? (Vincent Zuffante/Star File)

RICHARD SIMMONS

Most famous gig: Exercise videos; "Deal-A-Meal"; role on *General Hospital*; TV guest spots.

I am not absolutely certain who has appeared the most times on the Stern radio show, but Richard Simmons would be my first guess. No one has been picked on as much by Howard and company, and no one has stormed out of the studio as many times as Richard has. I'm not sure why he always seemed to come back, except that he considered Howard a good friend of his. That may have ended in 1993 when Howard talked about some tabloid allegations that Richard liked to be spanked by men. Howard even may have been the cause of the tabloid story, because he once said during a Simmons radio appearance, "I wish the *Enquirer* would put a full-time investigator on him" so Howard could find out what goes on in Richard's private life.

Each appearance by Simmons seemed to be an opportunity for Howard to see how far he could go before Richard would storm out of the studio. It really made for some great radio.

The typical Simmons appearance was marked by Howard's poking fun at Richard's effeminate voice and personality, his work with fat people, his body odor, his genitals (which he allegedly frequently flashed at Howard and the gang), his Barbie doll collection, his beloved dalmations, and his infatuation with Barbra Streisand. Well, no one ever said Richard was your typical guest.

Howard once told his audience—right before Simmons stormed out of the studio—that Richard was the type of guy "you just want to put a black leather hood over his head, stuff a rubber ball in his mouth, and put nipple clamps on him and squeeze him."

Once after having had Richard over for dinner the night before, Howard told how the exercise maven was attempting to get Howard's "father's phone number all night long" and how he said that he wanted to "spend a week alone" with Howard in a "log cabin." After Stern revealed that information on the air, Richard freaked out and yelled, "*Oh my God, no!!* You promised me that everything was sacred, and to you nothing is sacred."

Not that Richard didn't sometimes get in a dig at Howard. When Howard once called Richard's "Sweatin' to the Oldies" videotape "stupid," Richard hit him with this zinger: "Stupid? Stupid? You mean the video that is outselling yours by six million copies?" However, most of the time, the person that Howard once called "a perfumed, vicious man" was totally on the defensive.

Richard really does seem to care a lot about Howard's family—he has bought his daughters expensive Barbie dolls, cried when Alison had a miscarriage, and seemed honestly hurt when Howard told him he would not allow his daughters to spend a weekend with him by themselves. Howard told Richard, "I'd rather have them walk through Harlem with fried chicken on their heads." After Richard stated, "I am so humiliated," Howard added, "Thank God I don't have sons."

When Richard, whose original first name was Milton, made an appearance around the time of the Los Angeles rioting, Howard told his audience that Richard looted "four pair of stained undies from a Cub Scout meeting." In that same appearance, Howard, seemingly sensing something about Richard, told us, "If I spank him, he'll break right out of his shorts." Howard somehow was convinced that Richard "wanted" a spanking.

The thing that causes the most friction between the two,

though, was that Howard poked fun at the fat people Richard has devoted his life's work to. When a woman who said she weighed three hundred pounds called in looking for Richard's help, she was called "a big fatso," "a gargantuan mammoth," and "a big cow" in the span of thirty seconds. All the time, Richard was apologizing profusely to the woman for Howard's comments. That did not stop Howard from making a small (okay, large) wager with Richard: "You work on her left side, I'll work on her right side," he challenged, to see who could slim her down more quickly.

I think all of Howard's fans hope Richard comes back to the show. The two of them make radio magic together.

"TED THE JANITOR"

Most famous gig: Appearances on both the radio and TV versions of Howard's show.

Ted was really a janitor at the K-Rock studios in New York City. I guess it can be said that Howard discovered Ted while he was cleaning toilets, and soon after began putting him on the air. We all grew to love Ted's appearances. For those of you who do not know what Ted looked like, you can see him at the end of the "U.S. Open Sores" videotape. He also appeared on the old TV show as an Ethiopian who thanked Bob Geldof for his work with "Live Aid" and as Howard's father in the "Black Folks With White Features" segment, among others. His best work was on the radio, however, when Howard would have him come in and read bits they had written for him. Ted had a hard time reading and would usually just ad-lib through the bit.

Ted had had four heart attacks before the fifth one finally did him in. After his fourth one, Howard brought him into the studio to talk to him about it. Ted blamed the attack on a "Sicilian pie." Howard even talked about Ted's funeral with him during the visit. When he was asked by Howard whether or not he thought he would end up in heaven, he gave us a typical Ted response: "I don't know about no heaven, but when I come back I'm not coming as a chicken."

Ted was infatuated with Robin and let her know it at every opportunity. He was fond of telling her that he wanted to play "road" with her, and "pave you." When people told him that he was "crazy" for going on the Stern show, he would respond, "It might be crazy to you, but I have fun," or "There is nothing I could say wrong about Howard," or "He's great, especially him and Boobie [Robin]." You could tell Ted was having the time of his life whenever he was on the show.

As they always do, the Stern crew created a very touching tribute song for Ted, which Fred sang to the tune of "Desperado," called "Ted the Janitor." The song included, "God knows we really loved you and we'll always be thinking of you," as well as, "With you we had a great time, to leave so soon is such a crime." (Both this song and "The Sounds of Kinison" can really choke you up, and you can tell that the people who wrote them really cared about both Ted and Sam.)

After Ted's tribute song was played, one of Ted's eleven (yes, eleven) children called in to tell Howard and Robin, "He loved you guys." She added before hanging up, "You all extended his days a lot longer 'cause you made him really happy." Howard told her that he saw Ted as possessing "true happiness" and that the only thing he ever saw him upset about was "not getting Robin." Ted, we really miss you!

TINY TIM

Most famous gig: Singing "Tiptoe Through the Tulips."

Tiny Tim had all but disappeared from public view when he began to appear on the Stern radio show. He was surprisingly open with Howard and would explain all of his little idiosyncrasies, which included being ultraclean and addressing all women as "Miss." Unfortunately, a born-again Tiny became very upset on one last visit to the Stern show when he thought that Howard took the name of the Lord in vain. Everything was going smoothly on that visit until Tiny came to believe that Howard was "mocking Jesus Christ." Although I was listening that day I never could figure out what Howard said that set

Tiny Tim, *before* he became angry with Howard. (Pictorial Press Ltd./Star File)

Tiny off, but he really lost it, and you could feel Robin and Howard becoming real uncomfortable as Tiny yelled, "You're taking Jesus Christ's name in vain. . . . I reject that." Tiny Tim did not appear on the show for years after that. He finally came back to appear as a judge during the "Ms. Howard Stern" New Year's Eve show.

MEG GRIFFIN

Most famous gig: Disc jockey at K-Rock in New York.

Meg used to be the DJ who followed Howard Stern onto the airwaves at WXRK, and he would often have her come in early for a bit of friendly banter. Sometimes the banter would actually stay on an even keel, but more often than not Meg would begin to attack Howard, his crew, his show, his guests, his comedy, and his fans. Yes, that is right, Meg referred to us as the "idiots who listen to this program."

Ah, Meg, I've been waiting a long time to address that insult, which was directed specifically at me as well as Howard's millions of other listeners. You called me an "idiot" for listening to a program I get a ton of laughs and enjoyment from, yet it's obvious you not only listened to the radio show but also watched the old TV show, as you spouted off—verbatim—different bits that Howard had on both shows. These shows just got you angry and upset, yet you continued to listen and watch. Let's rethink just who exactly is the "idiot" here, Meg.

What exactly were Meg's problems with Stern and his

shows? (It might be a shorter list if we went over the things that were not a problem. I think the main issue in Meg's mind was Howard's treatment of women. After a particularly funny appearance by Sam Kinison and an entire entourage of scantily clad women, Meg told Howard, "It's Dante's Inferno in here," adding, "People like you are taking over the world; that's the damn shame of it." Another Megism that day: "Just because something's popular, it doesn't mean it's good." I disagree.

Don't get me wrong—I loved having Meg follow Howard, as did Howard. She was great for the show and offered Howard the opportunity to respond to some of the same inane arguments that are fired at him from the media, women's groups, and other people who say they hate him but can't find it within themselves to change the freakin' radio dial. Unfortunately, Meg may have done herself in with all her self-righteousness. She started refusing to do certain commercials at K-Rock, explaining, "I got better things to do than commercials" and "I won't put my voice on something I don't believe in." Meg was soon on a path of demotions; she now has to work the overnight shift at K-Rock.

Howard once pointed out to Meg the hypocrisy in her own brand of logic. She constantly condemned Howard for treating women badly, yet she made her living playing the records of bands, such as the Rolling Stones, Led Zeppelin, and Guns N' Roses, that, according to Howard, "have treated women abusively." Howard once asked her, "Who's left for you to play on your show . . . only Elton John." She condemns Howard, a family man who goes home to his wife and three daughters every day, because she doesn't comprehend that he does a *comedy* show, while she worships rock stars who use groupies like they are toilet paper.

Nevertheless, the Stern crew put together another one of their fine song parodies, featuring Fred Norris, backed by Pig Vomit, in order to pay homage to Meg Griffin. The song, sung to the tune of "Angry Young Man" and called "Angry Young Meg," points out the hypocrisy of Meg Griffin and all the do-gooders who think they know what's right and wrong for the rest of us. It tells how she "complains of pollution," yet smokes; how "Mick Jagger is her demigod," despite his womanizing; how she feels she has the right to urge Robin "to act black," even though she herself is white; how she is apparently so concerned with the poor, yet drives a "Beamer" (BMW); and how she won't do certain commercials, yet "cashes that paycheck."

I miss Meg and her battles with Howard. I miss Meg yelling "You're a Pig" and Howard responding "You know what—you're equally a pig." She really was a fabulous sparring partner for Howard, and we all enjoyed her zany logic. Without knowing it, she was the best example of the "closet fan" who spouts off how much he or she hates Howard, but can't turn the dial. I just hope she still finds time to listen to the Stern show now that she is on the overnight slot.

KENNETH KEITH KALLENBACH

Most famous gig: Attempting to blow smoke out of his eyes.

This is one of those guys who makes you ask, "Where the hell did Howard ever find him?" He was on one of the first episodes of *The Howard Stern Show* on TV and immediately became a hit when he attempted to blow smoke out of his eyes and ended up drooling all over the place. After that, he made numerous appearances and more attempts to blow smoke out of his eyes. On one attempt, he actually threw up (at least you know he was trying). After a while, the act started to get dated, so in order to show that he was versatile, he began to smear food on his face, light firecrackers in his crotch, cut off his hair and eat it, and do other fun stuff. Kenneth, who is a postal worker, even came up with a comedy routine, but it was so filthy, WWOR would not allow it to air. I may be paranoid, but if I worked in the same post office as Kenneth, I would consider wearing a bulletproof vest to work.

"RACHEL THE SPANKER"

Most famous gig: Spanking and performing the "Bronsky."

Rachel is here to represent all of the girls who show up at the K-Rock studios whenever Howard asks for girls to come down and take their clothes off for concert tickets, or to be Super Bowl massage girls, or just to have their breasts painted green for St. Patrick's Day. Rachel has been there for Howard on many occasions, including when he decided that he was going to have a "Nude Christmas Party" one year. For those of you who'd like to catch a glimpse of Rachel, she can be seen on the "U.S. Open Sores" videotape giving a "Bronsky" (where a man places his head between a woman's breasts while she flails them back and forth) to another Stern radio regular "Gina Man."

"SCOTT THE ENGINEER"

Most famous gig: Sound engineer at K-Rock.

Another staffer, but Scott Salem has also become a major part of the radio show. He is a constant target of Howard's because of his baldness and his cigarette smoking. Scott portrayed the bald Philadelphia Zoo Keeper during the funeral for John DeBella. He is constantly berated by Howard for not performing his job up to Howard's standards, and even had an award named for him during a presentation of the "FMies," which Howard passes out each year. The "Scott Salem Memorial Award" was presented to Gary one year for being the "best person who keeps a job in spite of his laziness, lack of drive, and abundance of bad habits." Howard explained why it's called "memorial award": "Scott's not dead, but how long could he possibly have left after all the cigarettes he smokes?" Although Scott takes a lot of abuse, he also gets a daily plug for his "mobile DJ service," which he started with a loan from Howard himself.

PENN GILLETTE

Most famous gig: Magician with partner Teller.

This very funny comedian-magician has been on the radio show many times and also appeared with Teller on the "Underpants and Negligee Party" videotape, where they proceeded to do their trademark blood-spurting magic. Penn is great on the show, but probably is best known by Howard fans as one of Robin's suitors. He lost out to soap opera star Michael Swan for an "FMie" for "Best Performance by Someone Trying to Bang Robin." (Robin calls her relationship with Mr. Swan, an actor on *As the World Turns*, "just a friendship.") Penn's nomination came from the fact that he left a message on Boy Gary's answering machine looking for Robin's phone number and asking her to call him. Apparently, a certain magician had a case of "jungle fever."

SUKHREET GABEL

Most famous gig: Testifying against her mother, Judge Hortense Gable, during a New York City bribery scandal involving Bess Myerson.

Sukhreet is here to represent all the people in the news that Howard somehow manages to have appear on his show. These include people like Joey Buttafuoco, Jessica Hahn, and ex-L.A. Police Chief Daryl Gates. Sukhreet not only was interviewed about her part in the political scandal that rocked the New York City political scene back in 1987, but also became Howard's official "Weather Girl" for a short time and makes a very brief appearance on the "U.S. Open Sores" videotape. I briefly spoke to Sukhreet about Howard, and she told me that she found him to be a very kind and pleasant individual. She stated, "Howard sent me flowers after my mother passed away."

DOUG JOHNSON

Most famous gig: Reporter for ABC in New York City.

Doug is here representing all the annoying reporters who hound Howard for a story, yet continue to produce the same old tired story, with no new angles. I was interviewed in 1993 by this elderly reporter for a segment he was doing about Howard Stern. It was supposed to be a two-part piece which would air on ABC in New York during "sweeps week." "Sweeps week" is when TV shows clamor to get Howard on the air to increase their ratings. Mr. Johnson was the failed morning host of a show that was the precursor to *Live . . . Regis and Kathie Lee.* He told me that he once had Howard on his show and that Howard, knowing the show had been canceled, proceeded to "trash" the set.

Anyway, Doug's Stern segment, which was hyped by ABC as a feature that would reveal something new about Howard, was just about the stupidest thing I've ever seen. As Howard stated on his radio program the next morning, it was a "rehash of every story we'd ever seen." Howard went on to call it a "half-ass report" from a man who'd had a "half-ass morning show" that Regis Philbin had had to take over in order to "save the day." He ended up berating Doug Johnson on the air for the report, which according to Howard also contained misinformation about his previous radio jobs and subsequent firings. On top of all that, the gray-haired reporter completely cut out my interview, which was an impassioned defense of Mr. Stern. Hey, but I did get to meet Kathie Lee and Frank Gifford, as *Live With Regis and Kathie Lee* is produced in the same ABC studio that my interview was held in. I'm sure if Kathie Lee had known that I was there to praise Howard Stern on camera, she might not have said "hello."

CAPTAIN JANKS

Most famous gig: Phony phone calls and harassing the Philadelphia Zoo Keeper.

The Captain's exploits concerning the Philadelphia Zoo Keeper are covered in detail in the Philly chapter (Chapter 4), but there is more to the good Captain than just being a thorn in the backside of the Zoo Keeper. He, along with the "Phony Phone Caller," and others has entertained us with some great calls into shows like *Donahue*.

Howard paid the Captain his highest praise when, during a Letterman appearance, he told David that Captain Janks was the guy "who started it all." Mr. Stern was referring to the starting of a grass-roots "campaign to get my name spread all across the country" via phone calls to various talk shows. Howard went on to talk about the time Ross Perot was being interviewed on *Today* when the Captain, or one of his imitators, called up and asked the onetime presidential candidate, "Would your mind meld with Howard Stern's penis?" Howard then attempted to talk others into trying out this newfound activity that is sweeping the nation. "There's a certain amount of power" that you have when you call up a show and mention Howard Stern's name, Howard commented to Letterman. "People are repulsed."

"CELESTE"

Most famous gig: Being infatuated with Howard and his show.

"Celeste" is a physically deformed frequent female caller to the show who will call for a "Dial-a-Date" with just about anyone. The really down-and-out Dial-a-Daters who can't seem to get to first base with anyone are in luck if they select Celeste as their date, and she lets them know it. I believe that her fantasy is to sleep with Howard, so instead she plays this out through others and everyone is happy.

TOM CHIUSANO

Most famous gig: Station manager at K-Rock.

I believe that Tom is officially Howard's boss at K-Rock, but it's very difficult to believe this, considering the way Howard has dressed Tom down on the air. Tom gets upset when Howard oversteps certain boundaries of good taste, but he really does sound like a good guy and never gets too upset with Howard's ribbing, at least not while on the air.
Tom is closing out this section of the "Who's Who" because he has been at K-Rock since Howard got there and has done a

good job of keeping the "King of Radio" reasonably happy. It is quite clear that the people at K-Rock value what Howard brings to their station. Thanks, Tom, and thanks to everyone at Infinity.

Well, that concludes this portion of the "Who's Who." Again, I couldn't include everyone, but I tried to list my favorites. If I left you out and you're upset about it, write a letter. If you're one of the people who refuse to do the Stern shows, you're missing the boat. Howard is fast becoming one of the most popular entertainment personalities in the industry, and you're missing an opportunity to reach millions of fans who hang on every word Howard and his guests utter. His is the ultimate show on which to plug a record, a movie, or a personal appearance, because Howard Stern fans don't just listen, they *support*. Just ask Patty Smyth, or anyone at Snapple.

THE LAST WORD: HOW TO REACH THE "KING OF ALL MEDIA"

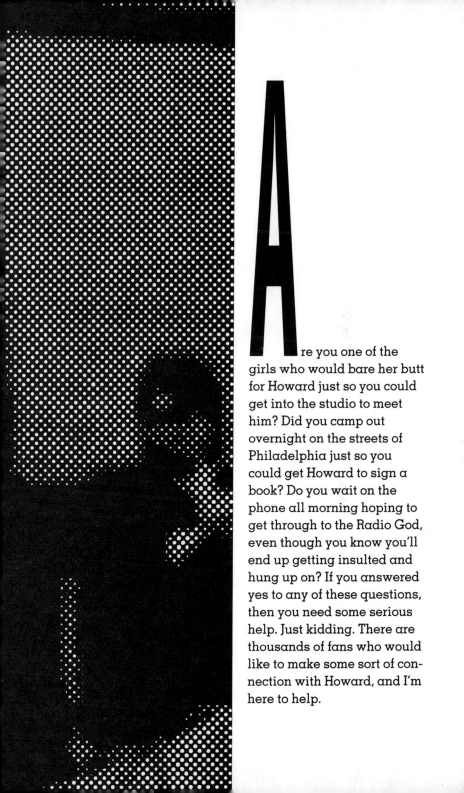

Are you one of the girls who would bare her butt for Howard just so you could get into the studio to meet him? Did you camp out overnight on the streets of Philadelphia just so you could get Howard to sign a book? Do you wait on the phone all morning hoping to get through to the Radio God, even though you know you'll end up getting insulted and hung up on? If you answered yes to any of these questions, then you need some serious help. Just kidding. There are thousands of fans who would like to make some sort of connection with Howard, and I'm here to help.

The "King of All Media" and his "Queen." (Fred Blake/Star File)

However, before I pass out any top-secret information, let me pass along some helpful hints for those of you who are inclined to call the *Howard Stern Show*. Here are some simple rules to follow:

1● Don't start the conversation by asking Howard, "How ya doing?" You'll be terminated immediately, and rightly so. We've been listening to Howard all morning; we know how the hell he's doing!

2● Have something relevant to say to Howard or don't bother calling. If you're calling to tell your friends you got to talk to Howard, you'll be off the air in a matter of seconds. So instead, while you're waiting on hold, give the matter a little thought and have something to contribute to the show if and when Howard picks up your line. Here are some ideas: this book, Rush Limbaugh, the big news of that day, a Sam

Kinison memory, your size 44-D luscious love lumps, your wife's size 44-D luscious love lumps, you heard Howard's name mentioned on *Larry King Live*, or your penis enlargement operation (this is a can't-miss option).

3● Don't hesitate to call him up to disagree with him on an issue. These are the best phone calls for the listening audience, as we get to hear you being chewed up and spit out. Here are some ideas for these masochistic Stern fans: Call up in favor of opening the borders of our country for the free flow of immigrants, call up to defend the "Right to Life" position, call up in favor of the verdict in the Reginald Denny trial, call up and say you're a huge Chevy Chase fan, or, for you real sickies, call up and say you're a member of the FCC.

4● Don't call him up to kiss his ass. He knows we all love him, and you won't win him over with a brown nose anyway.

5● Don't hesitate to call him up to talk about Robin's breasts, Gary's teeth, Jackie's cheapness, or Fred's weirdness. Howard never seems to tire of these subjects and they are your best chance of staying on the line for more than ten seconds.

6● Turn down your freakin' radio!! There is a seven-second delay and you will get confused trying to listen to yourself on the radio while talking to Howard. (How many fucking times does he have to tell you this!!!)

7● Call if you object to something he said. This will surely get you an audience with Howard, especially if you've got an indecipherable foreign accent, a speech impediment, or a debilitating physical abnormality. (In the last case, Howard may want to see you in the studio, or feature you on an upcoming video.)

When a phone call is utilized properly, it can be a listener's best opportunity to learn new things about his or her Radio

Go ahead, give them a call. I dare you. (Vincent Zuffante/Star File)

God. Such was the case when one caller asked, "Let's say you were in a pool of vomit and someone threw some feces at you—would you duck? Howard replied, "No, I wouldn't. I'd rather be hit by feces than actually duck myself in vomit." Of course, the caller got silly after his initial inquiry and Howard was forced to berate the guy before hanging up on him.

For those of you not brave enough to try and call Howard, you may want to write to him. You have a lot of options here. If you want to write for an autograph (I doubt you will ever get one, but you may get a publicity photo, gang autograph) or talk about the radio show, I suggest writing to K-Rock. Send him interesting articles, especially about himself or one of his other favorite topics, and he may do a "bit" around your submission. If you want to write to him about his TV shows, send your letter to E! Finally, if you want to mention his book, you may want to write to him in care of Simon & Schuster.

K-Rock
600 Madison Avenue
New York, NY 10022

E! Entertainment Television, Inc.
5670 Wilshire Boulevard
Second Floor
Los Angeles, CA 90036

Simon & Schuster
Rockefeller Center
1230 Avenue of the Americas
New York, NY 10020

For those of you who want to try and reach Howard on the phone, here are the appropriate phone numbers. Just remember, if you do get through, follow the guidelines posted above.

In New York, dial 212-955-9292. If you're calling from anywhere else in the United States, Canada, or Puerto Rico, just dial 800-44-STERN. Both of these numbers are for the studio; they are rarely answered. If you've got something important to say, call the K-Rock switchboard at 212-750-0550 and ask for the Stern show. You will then have to get through the "call screeners"—Baba Booey, Stuttering John, Gange, or Gorilla. But if you think you've got something that Howard would like to discuss, one of them will walk into the studio and tell him to pick up your line!

Finally, for those of you who want to fax Howard that nude photo of your wife and the family dog, just dial 212-759-KFAX.

AFTERWORD

Whether you like Howard Stern or not, it is clear that he's becoming an American icon. He isn't a flash in the pan, as a lot of the media would have you think. He's been around for a decade, and it is just now that his popularity is suddenly exploding. I think it's pretty clear that Howard is on the brink of superstardom when *TV Guide* asks Cher her opinion about the guy as part of an interview that has absolutely nothing to do with Howard Stern. Howard's radio and TV shows, books, and impending movie make him one of the few stars who have touched every facet of the entertainment medium.

The attacks on Howard by the FCC, NOW, and people like Donald Wildman are examples of the minority trying to infringe upon the rights of the majority. As Howard Stern fans, but even more so as proponents of free speech and the first amendment, we must fight these special interest groups and let the federal government know that it should not be spending our tax dollars on trying to silence a man who has every right to speak on the public airways. For those of you who do not have a sense of humor or simply don't like what he says, please just change the dial. Don't try to force your morality and personal preferences on the rest of us.

INDEX